What Good Is God?

Finding Faith and Hope in Troubled

Doug Herman

with Donna K. Wallace

Baker Books

A Division of Baker Book House Co
Grand Rapids, Michigan 49516

© 2002 by Doug Herman

Published by Baker Books
a division of Baker Book House Company
P.O. Box 6287, Grand Rapids, MI 49516-6287

Printed in the United States of America

Library of Congress Cataloging-in-Publication Data

Herman, Doug, 1961–
    What good is God? : finding faith and hope in troubled times / Doug Herman with Donna K. Wallace.
       p.   cm.
    Includes bibliographical references.
    ISBN 0-8010-6406-6 (pbk.)
    1. Suffering—Religious aspects—Christianity. 2. Consolation. I. Wallace, Donna K. II. Title.
    BV4909 .H47 2002
    231′.8—dc21   2002006673

For current information about all releases from Baker Book House, visit our web site:
http://www.bakerbooks.com

This book is dedicated to you;

the one who has selected it from the shelf and asks whether God exists or not, in the midst of pain unleashed equally on the innocent and the deserving, and in the midst of the aftermath is haunted by the lingering question . . .

"What good is God?"

Contents

Part 3. What Good Is God in My Failures?

Acknowledgments

The "thank-you" page is perhaps one of the most difficult ones to write in a book like this one. Donna and I have simply transcribed the book as it evolved in the lives of those who have touched us in the midst of their sufferings and celebrations. Our faith is strengthened and continually challenged by theirs.

We express our deepest thanks to the God of the storm, of life's tragedies, and our own personal failures, and to all those who keep us believing that God is good.

From Doug

My wife, Stephanie, has entered my office numerous times, speaking while turning the doorknob, only to get that glazed stare from me while deep in thought. Sweetheart, I'm sorry and I love you. Your insight, critique, and wonderfully sharp mind are my first source of reference. To my children, Josh, Bri, and Luc, you have made me smile and laugh and keep going. I love you and will make it up soon. I appreciate my extended family on both sides and also our small group family that meets every week; you've stretched me. Tina and Terry Jacobson, you mean more to me than you'll realize this side of heaven. Chip MacGregor, thanks for shooting straight—and for the chimichangas. Jack Nicholson, thanks for being real and rebuilding my faith in myself and God. Vicki, Dan, and the staff at Baker Book House, thanks for giving me the opportunity. And finally to Donna, I know no other woman as balanced with gritty determination and artistic expression. Thank you for your heart.

From Donna

As I look at the piles of books on my office floor, I realize again the privilege of gleaning from the finest writings of the finest men and women of history. As you scan our endnotes, remember my thanks to those who have gone before us.

In the long hours of writing, I have discovered anew the heart of God through the delight of my children, Cierra and Spencer, and the servant heart of God in the gentle, helping hands of my husband, Jamé. Thank you. My community and family are inseparable as they extend beyond the walls of our home. To all those so dear, know the Holy Spirit has encouraged and guided me through life's toughest questions in your tight embrace.

Doug, I am forever changed. Thank you. Your gift of passionate hope and growing trust gives me courage to move beyond "the gray zone."

⌒∾

The LORD is my shepherd, I shall not want.
    He makes me lie down in green pastures,
he leads me beside quiet waters,
    he restores my soul.
He guides me in paths of righteousness
    for his name's sake.
Even though I walk
    through the valley of the shadow of death,
I will fear no evil,
    for you are with me;
your rod and your staff,
    they comfort me.

You prepare a table before me
    in the presence of my enemies.
You anoint my head with oil;
    my cup overflows
Surely goodness and love will follow me
    all the days of my life,
and I will dwell in the house of the LORD
    forever.

Psalm 23

An Invitation

Few people anticipate walking the darkened path that winds through the valley of shadows. For it is in this valley that you find yourself tripping on the stones of unforeseen regret. Through the dark peer eyes of predators, who long for your failure that they may pounce and devour any remaining integrity or strength. Then come the chilling winds of discouragement, biting your face and howling through undiscovered canyons ahead.

It is tempting to turn around. Who wouldn't want to go back to the pasture and fruitful meadow of life? There friends play with careless abandon. The meadow is filled with safety and life. But you don't turn. Instead, you pull your coat tightly toward your neck and walk on.

Many of you walk realizing there is no return. Perhaps you find yourself in a season of suffering or pain. You have an ailment in your life. You feel "stuck" on this path. You also feel alone.

Others of you journey this path by choice. You press on to accompany another on this treacherous road. Your love for them holds you there. Exhausted and aching for your place in the meadow, you look into their eyes and refuse the comforts of home. As for the future, you have little time to wonder. You walk on, hand in hand.

Look down at that path for a moment. There are footprints there. This road has been walked before, yet not one person experiences exactly the steps you have taken or can know the ones you have before you. You must set each foot precisely in its place. You must walk on, and no one can truly know your ache. However, you need not walk alone.

I too know this path well. I walked my wife and two-year-old daughter down this road to the table at its end. There they found perfected peace as they entered the house of the Lord. Returning in grief, I had to journey this road back toward the meadow. Each boulder, howling wind, and twisted turn was retraced. This path of grief is well worn.

As I see you enter the valley of shadows, I leave the renewed comforts of the meadow to join you there. No one should walk alone. This book is our journey together. The questions are those asked by others and myself; you can still hear them echoing in the canyons. I extend my hand to you in this simple text. Walk with me. We will laugh. Most assuredly, we will cry. But my dear friends, know this too: We will end in hope. Because the path, although treacherous, leads to one who is good.

I know. I've seen his outstretched hand reaching for you.

Doug Herman
July 2002

The Tale of an Ancient King

"More soup, my lord?" asked the handmaid Khanea. Her soft round face and large doelike eyes glimmered in the evening sun cascading through the open window of the king's chamber. The king nodded slowly, and she turned with bowl in hand and headed for the kitchen.

King David lay there alone. His wife, Bathsheba, had gone to get his son Solomon. His breathing slow and labored, David realized he was near death. It wasn't that he was scared. Little scared the king. In fact, he was quite excited. This was a day to be cherished.

Down the hall, Khanea must have stumbled and dropped the spoon and bowl. His eyes closed, David heard the clanking, ringing sound of the utensils. It reminded him of a time decades ago.

"Is there not a cause? Can I even speak?" Young David left his obstinate older brother Eliab to try and rally another warrior. "Listen, you get to marry the princess, you receive a financial reward, and your family receives a tax exemption for life! Attack those Philistines! That giant is nothing so long as God is on our side!" Israelite soldiers one by one cowered from the task, returning to their porridge. Some threw insults at David, but they bounced off him like pebbles off granite. His heart raged within him. "This giant just defamed our God! Somebody . . . do something!"

The old king's mind raced forward.

The giant had declared a demonic prophecy to David. Outraged and filled with a warm strangeness, David threw the strap of his shepherd staff over his shoulder and reached in his pouch for a stone. Suddenly, David surprised himself as he began screaming a prophecy of his own. "I come against you in the name of the Lord Almighty. . . . I'll cut off your head. . . . All gathered here will know it is not by sword or spear that the Lord saves!" The giant growled loudly as he raised his spear. David ran hard toward it, swinging the stone in his sling. With a loud shout, David released his ammo, crushing the thick bony forehead of Goliath. Blood draining from his nose, the giant fell to his knees, then to his side. Standing over his kill, David fulfilled his vow. The roar of the Israelite warriors filled the sky. Running past him after the Philistine army, David heard them. "Atta boy, David!" "For David and for the Lord!" "What a shot!" "David, I'm here. David? David, are you okay?"

"David, I'm here. Are you okay?" The old king opened his eyes to see his beautiful wife, Bathsheba. He smiled, the crow's feet wrinkling from his bright eyes to his temple. She placed her hand on his and squeezed gently. In that moment, a lifetime of conversation traversed. "Solomon will be here shortly," she whispered.

Ah, Solomon. What a great son! David had placed him in the throne before God and the Israel assembly months earlier. The wisest and most compassionate of David's children, he would fare well.

Sitting quietly with his wife, David could hear the voices of his grandchildren playing beyond the portico. He closed his eyes and the curtain of his memory opened again to his childhood.

"David can't catch me! David is a sissy!" His older brothers loved to tease him. It seemed they would daily push him to the point of breaking—and that point came easily. "You take it too personally, David," his brother Abinadab complained. Shamah spoke up, "Sensitive little brother, don't let them put you down. Perhaps God has a plan for this tenderness . . . like becoming a nanny!" David growled and lunged for them both. But he always made up later. It was just how he was.

The youngest of eight boys, David actually enjoyed his role as the family shepherd. He practiced his music and swordplay on the hills beyond Bethlehem, the sheep as his audience. "You never know when I might need to protect my flock," David would say wryly to his family. Turning back to the meadow, with his long curly hair bouncing behind him, he'd run as fast as he could. There was something restful about being alone with God.

Khanea brought the soup back into his room and stood by Bathsheba. Still resting, David could smell the olive oil and the fresh bread on the tray.

"David! David! Come quickly!" shouted his brother. "Samuel the seer is in our home and wants to speak with you!" David threw his last stone at the large piece of bark with a bear head scrawled on it, hitting the bear's image in the eye. Grabbing his harp, David turned and began to run home. His legs churning clouds of dust behind him, he raced by his brother and into the house.

Still panting hard, David entered and walked up to Samuel. The old man looked strangely at David for only a moment. David's hair was matted and tied behind him; beads of sweat mingling with dust created crooked trails down his cheeks. Eliab, David's oldest brother, was the largest of the eight. David was smaller and thinner. The seer looked at each of the boys once more as if he were sizing them up for a war. Then a warm smile spread across Samuel's face. "God has chosen you, David." Taking a flask from his pouch, the seer and priest raised it over David's head. The warm olive oil ran down his hair, cascading over his face and shoulders and seeping into his clothes. Mother began weeping while his brothers gasped. This anointing was done only when choosing God's man—the next king. David's eyes danced wildly and he fought to remain motionless. The oil was warm. So very, very warm. As if . . . as if he could feel it running into his body and covering his soul.

The old king reached down and pulled his comforter closer to his neck. It felt cooler than before, and he longed for warmth. "Aren't you proud of our new king, David?" asked Bathsheba.

"He's a fine man. I'm so very proud of him," answered David in a whisper. "The third. He is Israel's third king . . ." He closed his eyes again and rested.

"You are the prince! Prince Jonathan, correct?" asked David boldly. "That's correct, friend! And you are the giant-killer." It was more of a statement than a question, so David answered only

with a dry grin. They greeted each other and looked into the other's eyes for a moment. Both had the energy of a stormy sky and knew that a good friend was vital in times of war.

Their friendship grew over the years. David's loyalty to Jonathan's father, King Saul, was unsurpassed. Even when the king's psychotic mood swings threatened David's life, forcing him to flee to the desert, David respected the king. Jonathan and David knew of David's anointing to become the second king. True to the heart, Jonathan was never jealous.

Jonathan vowed to remain devoted to his friend. "You must go. The king has vowed to kill you," Jonathan sadly shared. It was the last time David saw Jonathan before David had to flee for good. They hugged and wept for some time. They were brothers, unlike any relationship he'd had with his own blood.

When the report of Jonathan's death came to David, he wept the same tears that flowed in their good-bye. King Saul was killed in the same attack. The next king was to be announced by Samuel— David knew his time had come. Once on the throne, he wanted the blood of those Philistines who killed Israel's first king and his dear friend, the prince. Now the second king, David, would build a kingdom for his heir. "Solomon!" he called out.

Entering the room in his robe, the new king replied, "I am here, Father!" His strong voice reverberated in the chamber. David opened his eyes to see his son. Solomon knelt beside him reverently and lovingly. His shoulders were broad and muscled under the fresh linen, like the beams of a cedar in springtime. His dark neck angled up from his shoulders to his sharp jawline where his jet-black beard framed his smooth face. Unlike David's wild curls, Solomon had fine black hair like his mother's. Pulled back from his face, you could see his light brown eyes wet with tears. "Father? Are you okay?"

"You are here, son; of course I'm okay," David reassured. "I'm dying, mind you. But I'm quite all right!" David laughed, his laughter quickly turning to a hacking cough. Khanea ran to get some ointment from the desk. Seeing her, David motioned her to stop. "I'm fine, child. Leave an old man to die."

David lay back in his bed and rested again. "Bathsheba?" he asked.

"I'm here, my love," she replied, caressing his face and hair. *"My love? Is that you?" she asked.*

"It is," replied David. He was behind a curtain dividing his chamber from an outer room and came out to her. The king looked at her, melting from her beauty. Long dark hair flowed over her shoulders and down her rounded chest. Her eyes were a light brown, dancing in delight. She was the most beautiful of all the women the king knew. Her brow voiced concern.

"What are we to do now?" she asked.

David embraced her and held her close, smelling the jasmine in her hair. She was to be his wife soon, but only because she already carried his child. He truly loved her, but he ached with the deep secret that he had stolen her from one of his soldiers, Uriah. David had seduced her while Uriah fought for him in battle—where the king should have been himself. He had just been told that Uriah died on the front lines, so Bathsheba was his for the taking. He should be ecstatic; and he was . . . sort of.

Then Nathan, God's prophet, came to David and told a story of a rich man so greedy that he would take the only lamb his neighbor owned. "That man deserves to die," David responded angrily. "You are the man," Nathan said. David confessed his sin before God and was forgiven.

"May God be gracious to us and bless us," sang Solomon quietly. Bathsheba joined in. "And make his face shine upon us, that your ways may be known on earth, your salvation among all nations."

David's heart, trembling from the remembrance of his sin, quickly calmed. God had forgiven him and all was at rest. The king loved his God more than he loved any human. Those most endeared to him knew it and loved him all the more for it. There was no sight as majestic as watching the king sing and worship his Creator. Eyes closed, David lay on his bed listening to them sing the psalm. With raspy voice, he hummed along.

"May the peoples praise you, O God; may the nations be glad and sing for joy, for you rule the peoples justly and guide the nations of the earth. May the peoples praise you, O God; may all the peoples praise you. . . ."

They continued to sing together, although the king became deathly still. Bathsheba and Solomon embraced as they adored the face of the lover of Israel. Worshiping, David accepted his kingship. Worshiping, he relinquished it. Now face-to-face with the King of Kings, David worshiped, never to cease again.[1]

Introduction

Many of us were brought up to believe that it is wrong to question God. We wonder if it is safe to give voice to our honest questions of doubt and fear . . . or the anger that looms deep within our hearts. But we who have been in the quake of tragedy hurt so badly that we must speak out our pain and wondering to God.

I've come to believe that God is not offended by our questions. Tragedy threatens ministers just as anybody else. I too have had the comforts of doctrine and tradition stripped from me. Within the few short months that I lost my wife, baby daughter, brother, and grandfather, crisis after crisis ripped and peeled away the cozy blanket of theology and rituals that I had never before questioned. I was left with nothing but the skeleton of my faith—just enough to believe there was a God who would hear and answer my question.

"What good is God?"

Dare We Ask Such a Question?

Irreverence? Blasphemy? Even the sounds of these words have a bitter ring. Blasphemy sounds overly dramatic. I get a chill as

19

I imagine it bouncing and echoing off the high-pitched ceilings of cathedrals. Should we fear the results of our questioning?

We are faced with the evil of pain every day. The questions we ask are not rhetorical. I can't ignore them each morning as I open e-mail and answer the phone. Every single day broken people who are searching for hope approach me. Cancer patients, widows, and orphaned students look into my eyes, pleading, "Help us find answers, please."

I have two choices: Either I can bring these embittered questions to God, or I can turn a deaf ear to them. Either my spirit stays roused to their need, or my passion is snuffed out. My need to ask overcomes my fear of what answer I might receive. I know I might hear a harsh reproof, but I have to ask. If it's irreverent to ask if God exists, if it's wrong to ask if he feels this pain or if he cares, I must risk irreverence.

If God has any part at all in our story, I'm betting that he is all right with hearing about it. If a person is worried about the unforgivable, the fact that she is able to worry or question gives proof that her conscience is alive and not seared. God has not cast her away. The very questions that people fear are irreverent may actually be the ones that drive them closer to the heart of God.

If you have suffered, or have walked with one who has, you know how tempting it is to grow cold. Resentment indeed can yield to bitterness as we wrestle with bottom-line questions. When unfair circumstances or inappropriate responses of others stir up ugly passions, our souls lose freedom, spontaneity, and joy. If you are walking alongside a loved one who is suffering, you will be faced with some impossible questions, if you haven't been already. Our hearts are with you. We know the desert through which you walk: one full of questions, with seemingly few answers, little understanding, tons of demands, and loads of guilt for your own health or well-being. The suffering of others often awakens our own issues. *What Good Is God?* is for you too.

If you have purchased this book as a gift for a loved one, allow the hard questions to be asked. You don't have to answer them.

A Good Match

What Good Is God? offers solace through hard times, but it is not a turbo boost through suffering. This book offers room to ask the hardest questions. There's room for a wrestling match. It's not possible simply to *read* a book such as *What Good Is God?* No, my friend, you must *wrestle* this one!

"Without a question," says renowned spiritual director Henri J. M. Nouwen, "an answer is experienced as manipulation; without a struggle, help is considered interference. . . . Therefore, our first task is not to offer information, advice or even guidance, but to allow others to come into touch with their own struggles, pains, doubts, and insecurities, in short, to affirm their life as a quest."[1]

You will share the mat of experience with many other wrestlers, but your match, your story, is yours alone. The stories told here are real. You will find some tearstained faces within these pages, but each chapter also tells of victories won. In the words of Dr. Larry Crabb, "Tragedy is not the final word."[2]

Whether through pervading, silent wonder or raging anguish, "What good is God?" is a question that crosses boundaries and cultures: kings, beggars; men, women; old, young; ancient, contemporary. Questions in the midst of tragedy come in many forms: "Why would God allow this?" "Where is God in the midst of my pain?" "Does he even exist?" But these are birthed from one foundational question, "What good is God?"

What Good Is God? belongs with the daily newspaper, a cup of coffee, and a notebook or a friend. Instead of reading one page after another from cover to cover, use the contents page to navigate to the answers you need today. Our hope is that each chapter will be marked up with pages bent and the spine broken, sure signs of a good wrestling match.

Set aside quiet moments to let your heart beat with those whose stories are told here. Be still and allow yourself to process each circumstance. We hope you'll consider the ancient text and life of King David and be challenged by his honesty. We hope you too will risk being irreverent in your search to know truth. Recite or pray the words of the king's heart.[3] Interact with them and make them yours. They can awaken your spirit to your loved ones' needs as well as your own. They can be your prayer when you know of nothing else to do or say. May they bring you comfort and confidence that you don't have to fix the problems, but rather that you may "weep with those who weep and laugh with those who laugh." Walk together . . . and comfort with words only when you have to.

1

The Possibility of God

Sometimes faith is hazardous work. In transforming our heartaches to joy, we face doubts that nudge us uncomfortably close to unbelief.

Calvin Miller

The evening is dark and the townsfolk hunger for this hanging. The beautiful young gypsy Esmeralda is perched onstage, the hangman's noose taunting her smooth neck. Soon, all is still. A deathly hush falls over the crowded square. Weak and listless, Esmeralda breathes her last and awaits the hangman's fateful throw when suddenly a ghastly figure swings down from nearby scaffolding. Grabbing the girl from the noose, he sweeps her up toward safety atop the cathedral rooftop. Riotous yelling erupts as the avenging army plunges toward the doors of the Cathedral of Notre Dame.

The disfigured hunchback reaches the rooftop of the cathedral. Victoriously, he lifts Esmeralda's limp form over his head and screams, "Sanctuary! Sanc-tu-ary!"

The Great Escape

How many times will we narrowly escape our own demise? We turn and run with the pain and threats of the world closing in on us. We race inside our self-constructed sanctuaries and attempt to bar the door against our perils. Turmoil pummels the doors that we once believed were strong enough to hold harsh realities at bay.

Our defenses are faulty at best. We hear the pounding. Will the doors hold? Who feels secure enough to boldly yell, "I've found it! At last I've found sanc-tu-ary!"?

Humanity has sought escape in many forms. A couple of hundred years ago Marx said, "Religion is the opiate of the people." Needless to say, memorizing the well-worn quote helped us pass Philosophy 101, but Marx is now outdated. No, *escapism* is the opiate of the people who face a new millennium.

When we can't find a place of safety or reprieve, we settle for temporary escape. Gaining entrance to a world of fantasy is easy—the entertainment industry gives it to us in every imaginable form. Life is hard, we're tired, and we want a break.

Yet entertainment isn't enough. Chemical highs, sexual highs, and shopping highs just aren't enough. They are all temporary fixes at best. In the quiet we face a familiar nagging of emptiness. We can't help wondering if a place of eternal peace and safety truly exists.

When was the last time you asked, "What is life all about anyway?" A friend of mine recently exclaimed, "If there is no God, life is a really bad joke and I'm the punch line."

After a "successful" day at the office, at the close of Grammy award–winning entertainment, while the yacht pulls into the harbor . . . humanity is left wanting. "There is a restlessness in all of us that prods us to seek God," says Steve Fry.[1] Something deep within us yearns to be filled, to be held, to be secure.

> But in my distress I cried out to the LORD;
> Yes, I prayed to my God for help.

> He heard me from his sanctuary;
> my cry reached his ears.

Psalm 18:6 NLT

How do we find true sanctuary? Is it found in a physical place or at a level of consciousness? Can we find it in our own essence? Do we have to breathe a certain way, scale a mountain, cross the desert? Stereotypically, Western civilization has imagined God residing in a building like the Cathedral of Notre Dame. But when many of us go to the building we can't seem to find him there. The psalmist claimed that his cries reached the ears of God. Dare we believe that?

Okay, Who Let the Evil In?

We walked cautiously toward the hospital conference room. I opened the door for my wife and one-year-old son. Evon and I exchanged worried glances. Joshua, with his hands in ours, seemed oblivious to any potential threat. Seated at the table were my wife's gynecologist and a new doctor—an infectious disease specialist. After introductions, the specialist began, "Mr. and Mrs. Herman, in our testing of donated blood, we have discovered that one of the two units of blood given Evon, after your son's delivery, tested positive for the HIV virus. This virus will probably cause AIDS." After a seemingly eternal pause, he added, "Evon tested positive as well. I'm afraid there is no cure." Our secure little family had been invaded.

When Evon and I faced the earth-shattering news in the hospital conference room, we were as shocked as anyone else would have been. The doctor's message was simple and horrible: "I'm sorry, but your wife will die. You and your son are also in danger." As we drove home after that proclamation, the thought of what the future held tore through my mind. I began to hear a strange viral voice: "I'm going to kill you, Doug," it said. "I'm going to kill your wife, you, and even your little boy. Where is your God now?" Where *was* God? Where had he been during that blood transfusion that would eventually kill my wife? This tragedy invaded my thoughts, my choice of vocation, and of course, my family life.

We had been two innocent teenagers from the Midwest with our lives laid out before us; now we were adults battling for love, life, health, and faith. We felt we were fighting alone, that no one had ever battled tragedy in this way before. But that wasn't true. This war has raged on for centuries.

Who is exempt from adversity and tragedy? No one. I have ministered to thousands who have seen their lives explode in painful circumstance. I see their faces in libraries, churches, high schools, colleges, and at the mall. I see the empty, hollow, distant look of those in need. Sometimes our eyes meet.

> "Not that I am (I think) in much danger of ceasing to believe in God. The real danger is of coming to believe such dreadful things about Him. The conclusion I dread is not 'So there's no God after all,' but 'So this is what God's really like. Deceive yourself no longer.'"[2]
>
> C. S. Lewis

When life is really bad, what good is *your* definition of God? When trust is broken and bitter disappointments threaten to strangle our lives, our natural reaction is to grab the controls. God seems nowhere to be found. Many great "thinkers" reason that God is not a relational being after all. Much less disappointing is a broad concept of love mixed with large doses of positive thinking wrapped around our "essence." Others believe God is simply a "good" force within us. We can then decide when and how often to tap into the power of this force in order to live well. However, the question remains: What good is this god when things are bad?

Current Events

Something in this world is not quite right. Regardless of your definition of good or evil, bad is definitely on the rampage. If humanity carries the responsibility to care for Mother Earth and all the life she has birthed, shouldn't this be a happier place?

If the "force" within us is good, its power has somehow been short-circuited. Generations have failed, leaving humanity and the earth in deep trouble! We are born losers because pain and evil are everywhere.

We don't have to delve too deeply into theological discussion to ponder these things. All we need to do is open the front door or the front page of the newspaper. Perhaps a more striking headline crests your soul as you lie still in the quiet of the night. If suffering has not yet touched your life, wait. Soon enough you'll feel the raw ache of personal alienation or enter the suffering of others as you share life. There will come a time when you too will be staring pain in the eye.

> "There seem to be two kinds of people: Those who face the pain and those who hope it will just go away."
>
> Author Unknown

What type of person are you? Since you have picked up this book, most likely you have taken on the courage to face the pain. The reality of suffering brings us to a question that even precedes our title question. We can't ask, "What good is God?" until we've considered the possibility of God. We must first ask, "Who or what is the source of all that is, the giver of life?"

Have you ever wondered why we shake our fists at the sky in times of peril? Why do we curse, swear, or make vows by the name of God? If we stop to ponder these big questions, we sink into further wonder. We question even deeper until we finally ask, "Why am I here? What is the purpose of all this?"

Philosophy asks, "If a tree falls and no one is there to hear it, does it make a sound?" I ask, "If you are alone in the dark and you cry out, does a god hear you?" Have you ever wondered . . . When I am crouched in a corner as my drunk father hits my mom. . . . When my company merges with the large corporation that eliminates my position, reducing me to a job portfolio. . . . When my child lies in a sterile hospital bed with her face distorted by the life-essential tubing. . . . *Does anyone care?* If there is a God, what good is he to me now?

Does this ruler of the universe deserve our devotion when he/she/it refuses to end the evil peril and disaster of the world? Yes, God's existence does matter in times of hardship and suffering.

What Good Is Religion?

Many of us between the ages of twenty and fifty struggle with losing sight of a loving, merciful God in the cloudy disillusionment from church dogma and ritual.

Our parents seemed happy enough with religion. Religion and politics were passed down with the family heritage. Sadly, just as many parents spoke about religion without ever really living it. I feel like a minority, because I am one of the few whose parents are still married and living their faith. Many of my friends come from religious homes that have been split down the middle by divorce. "Ha!" they exclaim, "God must have stayed at church, because he never visited my house!"

No, we won't settle for a faith that doesn't make a difference each day. Faith means trust, and we have learned our lesson well: *Never trust completely.* It's no wonder we take our spirituality into our own hands. We need a faith that works in our lives as a whole. Sadly, for many hurting people, churches and their routines mean little more than elegant settings for baptisms, blessings, and burials.

Pointing our fingers at the church is much more comfortable than dealing with our own egos; it's much easier than lifting the shades that shield dark corners of our souls. Those who search for *the truth*, not relative truth, will be set free. Yet few are willing to face the dark painful truth of their aloneness and suffering.

Knowing truth and being free—isn't this exactly what we are looking for? Jesus said the truth will set us free, not that truth *is* free. It is sometimes costly and does not necessarily come wrapped in a life of ease or happiness. I found truth on life's anvil of seemingly unbearable events. After years of hammering, it stands the test of time. You see, *truth* is absolute.

Christian Pain

We all know that Christians do indeed suffer and experience pain just like anyone else. However, it is also true that Christians find the comfort of God in the midst of their tragedy. Even as a Christian in times of deep anguish, I am tempted to turn inward, to stomp away angry, and to "white-knuckle it" on my own. Soon bitterness begins to take over. I feel isolated and alone. I quickly become desperate. I know I must turn toward God or I'll start to die from the inside out.

> "Come to me, all you who are weary and burdened, and I will give you rest."
>
> Jesus of Nazareth

Not only did the evil of tremendous suffering rampage my life, it trashed my home. My wife suffered from the HIV virus, and we had conceived another child. Ashli was born an AIDS baby. Both Evon and Ashli suffered terribly before dying within eight months of each other, leaving me with a little boy to raise alone.

I pondered whether or not God existed. I guess, at that point, God seemed of little good to me. For months I found no rest, no peace anywhere. With countless questions in my soul, I refused to stop digging until I hit truth. Exhausted and spent, I found myself back in the original place I had known to find rest, the only place where perfect love is promised me—at the heart of my Creator. The perfect model of a parent, God stayed with me in my search.

I had cried and prayed and screamed so hard, there were times I had no words left of my own. In these moments I found comfort in lyrics from those who knew pain like mine—words that spoke my heart's cry.

King David's God

Like the contemporary musicians and artists who depict raw pain and dare to look life square in the eye, the ancient writer King David held nothing back. He hammered God with questions daily. He was confident of God's love for him as a child is certain of her parent's love. David returned again and again to speak his mind to God.

Most often King David began his monologue in outrage and angry wonder—shaking his fists at the sky, pacing, and sharpening his sword—his brow beading in sweat as to why God allowed the attacks upon his life and character.

David's prayers often closed in sharp contrast; he collapsed, his hands lifted in worship, and he relinquished his deepest concerns. Breathless, he knelt in quiet resolve and praise of the one true God. "Teach me your way," whispered the king, "and I will walk in your truth; give me an undivided heart. . . . great is your love toward me; you have delivered me from the depths of the grave" (Ps. 86:11–13).

"Great is your love toward me," said King David. Isn't it fascinating that humanity is born with an innate knowledge that love is good? We cannot know good apart from love. We therefore cannot possibly know God is good apart from the reality of his love for us. What good is God when life is really bad? May we discover the God who lavishes his favor on us in the midst of a broken world so we can be free from rejection and abandonment, for the truth of God's great love is our sanctuary.

> "What we believe about God is the most important thing about us."
>
> A. W. Tozer

I have found that God not only provided an abstract understanding of love for us, but his love is most perfectly demonstrated in the life of his Son, Jesus. Though my personal faith has been stretched by many difficult questions and the old traditional answers have been deeply challenged by suffering, and though I have questioned and yelled at God in my darkest hours, I *know* God's love for me. I have never been alone. My deepest sufferings were shared and understood by Jesus.

"To say with all that we have, think, feel, that 'God exists' is the most world-shattering statement that a human being can make," claims Henri J. M. Nouwen. When we make such a statement, all intellectual, emotional, and spiritual understanding becomes clear and only one truth remains: God exists. "Because God exists, all that *is* flows from God."[3]

Communicating with This God

It is no simple task to communicate with a God we can't see. He is spirit. Yet so are we. If we stop running toward escape long enough, we can acknowledge that we live in both body and spirit. "We know that we live in him and he in us, because he has given us of his Spirit" (1 John 4:13).

We attempt to live a life fully embracing our intellect, our spiritual life, and our physical reality. Prayer ties all these things together. Very simply, prayer is our dialogue with God about life. It is words, thoughts, actions, reflections, motives, and attitudes—all that lies closest to the heart. Here we begin to experience the difference between *believing* and *knowing* God. "Knowing God is not an optional extra, but an essential part of what it means to be human. We are not fully alive until we are alive to God and in touch with him."[4]

The symbol of the heart "captures the deepest essence of our personhood," says Brennan Manning, author of *Abba's Child.* "It symbolizes what lies at the core of our being; it defines who we really are. We can know and be known only through revealing what is in our heart."[5] To know God we must open our hearts by asking the honest questions and allowing ourselves to be found by God. When we seek God, he finds us. His truth will resonate and flow through our life, making us fully alive.

Will you only settle for fantasy and a temporary escape, or do you seek truth and sanctuary? This is the choice you have before you. Many paths involve escape. You can easily believe there is no God and rely on your own strength and finite knowledge. Or you can choose a path toward God, who offers a sanctuary of perfect love and mercy. His path, though not always clear to us, offers eternal companionship. He never leaves us to journey alone.

You can be free and content. Jesus said, "I will never leave you nor will I ever forsake you." I can confidently say, "God is my help. I will not be afraid. What can men do to me?" (Heb. 13:5–6).

Take a chance and let God hold you silently against his heart. In learning who he is, you will discover who you are. God has

shown through many Scriptures that he longs to communicate
with his creation. God says to us, "Call to me and I will answer
you and tell you great and unsearchable things you do not
know" (Jer. 33:3).

"Do not be carried away by varied and strange teachings" (Heb.
13:9 NASB); rather pour out your heart to God, as the psalmist
did, for God is our refuge (Ps. 62:8, paraphrase). Even if you don't
fully believe in God and still have many questions regarding the
life of his Son, Jesus, remain open to the meditative prayers of
King David. They begin beautiful healing, bring immediate comfort, and draw a person's heart toward God over time.

An unknown author of the fourteenth century wrote a book
entitled *The Cloud of Unknowing*. Even the title of the book
sums up what we often feel in our walk through life. The wisdom of the mysterious sage is a favorite of many:

> Do not give up . . . when you first begin, you find only dark-
> ness and as it were a cloud of unknowing. You don't know what
> this means except that in your will you feel a simple, steadfast
> intention reaching out toward God. . . . Reconcile yourself to
> wait in this darkness as long as is necessary, but still go on
> longing after him.

> *Hear my prayer, O LORD;*
> *listen to my cry for mercy.*
> *In the day of my trouble I will call to you,*
> *for you will answer me.*

> *Among the gods there is none like you, O LORD;*
> *no deeds can compare with yours.*
> *All the nations you have made*
> *will come and worship before you.*

> *. . . you alone are God.*[6]

>   Psalm 86:6–10

Part 1

What Good Is God in Life's Storms?

In this first of three sections, we find ourselves asking a brash question. Storms come and deeply impact humanity world-wide. "Acts of God," we call them. They can hit with surprising force, sending us into shock and survival mode.

When the rains subside and the rubble clears, we begin rebuilding. However, something remains in our souls beyond the refurbished walls of our homes and offices. In the aftermath, we ask, "What good is God in the storms?"

If God is truly all-powerful and all-knowing, why didn't he calm the storm? If God isn't all-powerful, then what kind of God do we have?

We must be honest with our questions. Let us link arms and walk in open-mindedness. The questions are deep and troubling. But we can be assured that there is an answer to be found, and we shall continue walking until we find the truth.

May God guide our sincere thoughts and questions. May that path lead to truth and hope.

2

Is God Truly Safe?

Hardships press us up against God.

Joni Eareckson Tada

Safety. Ah, the thought! Wouldn't it be sublime to rest in complete safety and peace? And how marvelous it would be to never again experience sickness, to wake up and walk each day in complete assurance that tragedy and pain have forever been obliterated.

Sadly the world does not offer such bliss. Things go "bump" in the night. Each day we wake up to a life of uncertainty. We struggle to find safety, trying to create it in our homes with locks, blinds, and security systems. We pay absurd amounts of money to insure our possessions, our health, even our life. Fear often stalks us as we walk our children to school, as we battle for a safe environment that wards off evildoers.

Evil has infiltrated the world, and it is not safe. From the moment we are born, we begin to learn how to protect ourselves, fight off sickness, and carry financial burdens. Still Christians live in poverty, get sick, and die. What good then is the God who promises he will hear us from his sanctuary? No one wants false security.

Yes, God offers companionship, rest, and peace in the midst of trials. But is God truly safe when he allows catastrophes that annihilate entire populations? For those of us who believe in God as our Creator and Parent, involved in our lives and concerned about our well-being, these questions arouse much more than intellectual doubt. Our faith or trust revolves around a crisis in personal relationship. If God is personally involved in our lives, he takes a position of great relevance—he is living with us in our world, not only in our minds or metaphysical encounters.

Does God deserve our trust, no matter how hard the winds are howling? Is the sovereign hand of God ever lifted? Does he ever turn his back? How can God be all-good, all-powerful, all-knowing, yet allow colossal tragedy to occur? In the wake of calamity, many discount the existence of God.

"Mr. Herman, I cannot believe in your concept of God. If I believe in a God, then I have to believe that he is all-powerful. And if I truly believe *that*, then I struggle with God's goodness as I watch people reeling in the aftershocks of natural disasters, in the devastation left in the wake of war, and the global suffering and unfairness of this world! How can anyone trust a God like that?"[1]

Have you ever felt this way? I have. I have wrestled many rounds with questions like these! Come with me deep into the struggle. From there, we will journey toward hope and resolve.

Lisbon, Portugal

It was a beautiful Sunday morning. The young boy threw open the door to his cottage and raced his older sister to the horse and buggy Papa had prepared earlier. "I win!" screamed Sister, edging past her brother to touch the carriage first.

As they clamored into the backseat, Mother and Papa exited the house. Mother had her little baby snuggled tightly in a warm blanket. Papa helped Mother to her place in the buggy before he climbed in. The sun shone bright on this cool and crisp day in November on All Saints' Day.

When everyone was situated, Papa took the reins and clicked his tongue. The old mare gently clopped down the familiar cobblestone road to Saint Paul's Church in Lisbon, a journey faithfully made every Sunday since the year Mother and Papa had married.

The smell of harvest was in the air, and the people on the street waved cheerfully. With a melody of little birds singing their morning songs, the children hummed a tune in rhythm to the clip-clop of the horse's hooves on the cobblestones. They passed stalwart trees lining the sunbaked road, hard-packed from years of commerce and trade. The buildings with their ancient designs stood harmonious with the new construction of the past several decades. Lisbon had become a successful and affluent city of some 250,000 residents. The capital of Portugal, it had grown to be one of the most prominent cities in all of Europe.

The grand buildings of Lisbon appeared even mightier as the family's horse and buggy approached. The salty smell of the ocean lingered in the air as they neared the river inlet and turned north. Mother always loved to see the ocean because it reminded her of "the vast strength, peace, and stability of God Almighty." On the other side of the river they could see the sun reflecting on the marble quay.[2] Not every city in Portugal had such stately piers to welcome those on the waterfront.

They passed by the famed opera house. Looking at the luxurious design of its walls and the large windows and archways reminded Sister of stories told of Rome's colosseum. The night before, the opera house had been packed for a performance.

Down the way they could see the patriarchal and castlelike Cathedral already filled with parishioners for early mass. They passed Saint Roch Tower where birds were already chasing and dancing with one another. Saint Nicholas's Church, which loomed some forty-five feet in the air, was the final landmark before they arrived at their home of worship, Saint Paul's Church. Tradition was of great value in this large extended family, and all the aunts, uncles, and cousins attended the same church.

As they arrived at Saint Paul's, Mother took the children to their classroom. Papa tied up the mare and shook hands with other men as they entered the building. It was nearly 9:00 A.M. The year was 1755.

Finishing a letter before morning services, Reverend Charles Davy described the morning from his apartment study: "There never was a finer morning seen than the 1st of November; the sun shone out in its full luster; the whole face of the sky was perfectly serene and clear."[3]

At half past nine that morning, people congregated in various church buildings. On All Saints' Day, the cathedrals were filled with parishioners honoring the many saints with a multitude of lighted candles and prayers. The faithful studied Scripture and sang songs of praise to the Creator. They crowded Saint Paul's Church, Saint Nicholas's Church, and the Cathedral. Then it hit.

The first of three earthquakes struck the city with such force and surprise that many didn't even know what it was. "I was just finishing a letter, when the papers and table I was writing on began to tremble with a gentle motion," wrote Reverend Davy sometime later. "Which rather surprised me, as I could not perceive a breath of wind stirring. Whilst I was reflecting with myself what this could be owing to, but without having the least apprehension of the real cause, the whole house began to shake from the very foundation, which at first I imputed to the rattling of several coaches in the main street, but on hearkening more attentively, I was soon undeceived, as I found it was owing to a strange frightful kind of noise under ground, resembling the hollow distant rumbling of thunder."[4]

It had been two centuries since Lisbon had experienced such a shake as this. Inhabitants were stunned and dumbfounded, as the concept of "earthquake" had not yet been conceived. Reverend Davy continued, "Upon this I threw down my pen and started upon my feet, remaining a moment in suspense, whether I should stay in the apartment or run into the street, the danger in both places seemed equal. The house I was in shook with such violence, that the upper stories immediately fell; and though my apartment (which was the first floor) did not then share the same fate, yet everything was thrown out of its place in such a manner that it was with no small difficulty I kept my feet, and expected nothing less than to be soon crushed to death, as the walls continued rocking to and fro in the frightfulest manner, opening in several places; large stones falling down on every side from the cracks, and the ends of most of the rafters starting out from the roof. To add to this terrifying scene, the sky in a moment became so gloomy that I could distinguish no particular object."[5]

The shaking lasted ten minutes and was felt as far away as Finland, suggesting a magnitude approaching 9.0.[6] Reverend Davy continued, "I hastened out of the house and through the narrow streets, where the buildings either were down or were continually falling, and climbed over the ruins of Saint Paul's Church to get to the river's side, where I thought I might find safety. Here I found a prodigious concourse of people of both sexes, and of all ranks and conditions, among whom I observed . . . principal canons . . . several priests . . . ladies half dressed . . . all these whom their mutual dangers had here assembled as to a place of safety, were on their knees at prayers, with the terrors of death in their countenances, every one striking his breast and crying out incessantly, *Miserecordia meu Dios! (Have mercy my God!)* . . . In the midst of our devotions, the second great shock came on and completed the ruin of those buildings which had been already much shattered."[7]

Certainly the air was filled with the manic screams of the disoriented, the moaning of those thousands partially crushed by sacred sanctuaries. Many people ran to the ocean shore to escape the continued collapse of rubble and debris. They arrived there only to find a tsunami forming in the ocean depths.

"In an instant there appeared, at some small distance, a large body of water, rising as it were like a mountain. It came on foaming and roaring, and rushed towards the shore with such impetuosity, that we all immediately ran for our lives as fast as possible; many were actually swept away, and the rest above their waist in water at a good distance from the banks."[8]

Tired, stunned, and battered, many ran for safety to the quay. It was built entirely of marble at an immense expense. Yet it too "was entirely swallowed up, with all the people on it, who had fled thither for safety, and had reason to think themselves out of danger in such a place: at the same time, a great number of boats and small vessels, anchored near it (all likewise full of people, who had retired thither for the same purpose), were swallowed up, as in a whirlpool, and nevermore appeared."[9]

~

What stirs within you after reading the accounts of Lisbon's tragedy? If you are at all like me, you feel sick. There resides a nauseous knotting in our stomachs. We are emotionally chilled as it either threatens our belief in protection or our denial regarding the possibility of danger. We feel vulnerable . . . unsafe.

Now picture in your mind a God who knows all. Envision a God who is all-powerful. He is a God who knew in advance this would happen. He watched as it occurred. He is a God who *could have stepped in*. But apparently he did not. So my question stands, "Is God truly safe?"

To be painfully honest, I believe the answer is . . . no.

God is not safe *as you and I perceive safety*. Do you disagree? Ask those parishioners on Saint Catherine's Hill who screamed, "Mercy!" to God. They watched as their loved ones were swallowed into the earth's abyss or were swept away by the sea. They heard the abrupt halt of screams as neighbors were crushed under the thundering mass of rubble, entombed under collapsed cathedrals they themselves built for God. He did not offer safety or rescue them from death in that moment.

I must confess that believing God is "not safe as we perceive him" is unnerving to me, but what am I to say? If God *is* safe, then who is to blame? Is it a lack of faith for those who perish? Is sin being punished? Are there freak acts of nature beyond God's control? No.

Though I am often tormented by my desire for God to step down and "make it all better," I am acutely aware of the danger of trying to manipulate Scripture to make God more palatable in history. We must accept this truth: God chose not to rescue people from impending peril in those instances. His infinite ways are beyond our finite understanding.

Storms

Storms are not only caused by the crashing and colliding of heat and cold in the atmosphere; they can just as likely be the clashing of individual differences in selfish ambitions. Sometimes natural tornadoes threaten less danger to our lives than do domestic disputes in the living room.

Turmoil, whether in physical nature or in our day-to-day living, is nothing new. The question "What good is God in the midst of life's storms?" is explored in the ancient writings of King David.

> My heart is in anguish within me;
> the terrors of death assail me.
> Fear and trembling have beset me;
> horror has overwhelmed me.
> I said, "Oh, that I had the wings of a dove!
> I would fly away and be at rest—
> I would flee far away
> and stay in the desert;
> I would hurry to my place of shelter,
> far from the tempest and storm."
>
> Psalm 55:4–8

This king of Israel, God's favored one, experienced intolerable strain. He longed for escape, for safety far from the tempest and storm. In a sense, he too screamed *"Miserecordia!"* to the heavens.

We can't imagine that a good God would allow hellish moments, but he does.

Enduring Hellish Moments

The term *hell* is used so often and loosely, it has all but lost
its powerful reality in our vocabulary. I don't wish to engage in
deep theological debate here. At the risk of sounding *irreverent,* though, I'd like to reframe hell just a bit for our discussion.
Many Christians believe hell is a literal place created for the
"evil one" and his followers at the end of time. That is not what
I want to talk about here (though I am not discrediting it or
taking it lightly). I would like to discuss instead those experiences that give us a temporal taste of what hell may be like.

We were not created to be isolated by pain, trouble, or relational brokenness. Isolation separates us from others and from
God. Therefore, when we experience such suffering, we do in
fact experience a taste of hell. Ultimately, hell is the final separation from all that is good and true and loving: God.

We were designed to live in a perfect "Eden," in intimate relationship with God and humanity. Many terrible things have
happened since, separating us from perfect love. I believe Christ
came to repair the great tearing that took place, the tearing that
ripped us from the Holy Presence, the cloak of God, our Creator. The Holy Spirit seals us from spiritual danger, but we are
still vulnerably exposed to physical and emotional evil and danger. For this reason, we endure hellish moments.

A Taste of Heaven

I believe also that the taste of heaven we experience here
on earth is directly related to our levels of shared intimacy
with ourselves, others, and most importantly, with God. How
often we return to the cloak that was ripped away—where we
are known, loved, and held close—determines the heaven we
experience now. Here our spirits can rest secure. But the best
we can hope for in our little chronicle of physical life is brief
glimpses of lasting love through human closeness. At best,
our human love is a blurred reflection of the more radiant
love of God.

"Knowing we belong to God is something we must trust," says Nouwen. "God is greater than your mind or your heart."[10] We must realize that when we come to "the end of the line [our life]," it is simply "the return home." We return to the space where we are so safely held . . . under the cloak of God. Somehow we can know that we belong in that embrace, that we are rooted in that first love.

King David knew that embrace in the midst of hellish times. Though he had been anointed as God's chosen king, David knew what it was like to be betrayed and later stalked like an animal. His predecessor, King Saul, had become insane with jealousy and hatred and plotted for many years to murder David.

In his desperation David cried out to God for his protection lest he "go down into the pit." Time and time again, David was at the hands of his enemies. Yet he still found hope and peace and goodness in the heart of God. He knew he was God's precious one. David was chosen and blessed. He also knew that he had to shut out all the storms and enter again into a sanctuary of meditation so he could hear God speaking to his innermost being: "You are mine. You are in my hand." *David found God to be safe, though his life under God's direction was rarely safe.*

For us to equate our physical safety with God being *safe* is to err in self-centered human perspective. We struggle with our limited understanding. Because we live in a world that recoils in the ripple effect of sin and being torn from the cloak of God, we will always live in peril and pain. My late wife, Evon, reckoned with this seeming injustice of life. "We live in a sinful world, and we often reap the fruit of that sin," she explained during an interview about her HIV infection received from a simple blood transfusion.

To be safe physically and to find safety with God can be two quite different dynamics.

In C. S. Lewis's much-loved classic, *The Lion, the Witch, and the Wardrobe,* a wonderful exchange takes place that illustrates for us a trust found in a seemingly unsafe God. The story finds Lucy and the other children at Mr. and Mrs. Beaver's house while they are searching for their missing brother, who is under the spell of the evil White Witch. In hushed tone, they are discussing Aslan the Lion, who symbolizes Christ, the God-man.

> Wrong will be right, when Aslan comes in sight,
> At the sound of his roar, sorrows will be no more,
> When he bares his teeth, winter meets its death
> And when he shakes his mane, we shall have spring again.[11]

And now a very curious thing happened. None of the children knew who Aslan was any more than you do; but the moment the Beaver had spoken these words everyone felt quite different . . .

"Is—is he a man?" asked Lucy.

"Aslan a man!" said Mr. Beaver sternly. "Certainly not. I tell you he is the King of the wood and the son of the great Emperor-Beyond-the Sea. Don't you know who is the King of Beasts? Aslan is a lion—*the* Lion, the great Lion."

"Ooh!" said Susan, "I'd thought he was a man. Is he—quite safe? I shall feel rather nervous about meeting a lion."

"That you will, dearie, and no mistake," said Mrs. Beaver, "if there's anyone who can appear before Aslan without their knees knocking, they're either braver than most or else just silly."

"Then he isn't safe?" said Lucy.

"Safe?" said Mr. Beaver. "Don't you hear what Mrs. Beaver tells you? Who said anything about safe? 'Course he isn't safe. But he's good. He's the King I tell you."[12]

You see, like the lion Aslan, God is not safe. But *he is good.* The sovereign God who holds the planets and the expanse of the sky in place holds the details of our lives in his hand. His ultimate good for you and me involves a plan that is much larger than our temporal situation. This plan encompasses all of creation. And . . . he is the King!

Henri J. M. Nouwen's entire life message held at its core the understanding that "We are created in and for all of eternity." What does this mean? Though we often feel trapped in the rubble of life, we must be mindful of our lives being only a section of time in the midst of an eternal plan. In the great expanse of time and humanity, these moments of agony are only *temporal hell.*

My friend, have you found yourself in these moments of fear? Perhaps you have such inner anguish that your soul nearly bursts with anxiety. Do you find yourself constantly on the brink of collapse from fatigue? If so, I have hope for you. On a path toward inner comfort and rest, King David left us some markers to follow. Continue with me as we learn from this ancient king.

A Path toward Safety and Rest

> In the day of my trouble I will call to you,
>   for you will answer me.
>
> Psalm 86:7

Here is the first marker on our path to hope: *We can call out to God*. You see, we are not alone on this journey. Though friends and family can accompany us physically, they cannot walk with us spiritually. Only God can abide with us.

"His presence flows into individuals who align themselves with Him; God's Spirit, an invisible companion, works from within to wrest good from bad."[13] In this journey, we can have a whisper of a thought . . . and God is there. Because he *exists*, the pleasure of deep companionship is brought to us. His very presence offers us a place to turn.

In the face of natural disaster, David had confidence in God's love for him. He found God to be good, as God provided hope through eternal safety even amidst a temporal hell on earth.

> Evening, morning and noon
>   I cry out in distress,
>   and he hears my voice.
>
> Psalm 55:16–17

Second, *God hears us when we call*. Certainly you have been in conversation with a friend, who, while you talked, had that glazed-over look on his face. When you stopped and called him to attention, he said, "I'm listening. Go on." But you knew better. His ears may have been functioning, but he never *heard* you.

God hears us when we call to him. When our heart is full of question or pain, he is there for us to turn to him. And when we express our deepest emotion . . . *he hears it all!* He will not turn a deaf ear. Never will we receive that glazed look. God longs for the intimate exchange from our souls to his too.

Our final marker is *trust*. Our earlier question remains: Can we trust a God who is not safe? Most would say no. However, remember, we must qualify the definition of safety. God is not safe as you and I perceive safety. Our perception is limited. Who can trust a God who seems dangerous? God, the Creator of the universe, is huge, holy, mysterious . . . and good. We fear him because of his power, but not because he is dangerous.

Danger connotes that he cannot be trusted because he might harm us. But God will not harm his children. Though harm may come as a result of a world clenched in the grip of evil, God is the model of perfection in parenthood. He will hold us secure. He enters into our moments of crisis. God often redeems tragedy while molding or disciplining us, reminding us of his great love. Our Father will direct us and will finish the good things he has begun. He has set eternity in the hearts of humanity; yet we cannot fathom what God has done from beginning to end (Eccles. 3:11).

The Bible says we "have redemption"—but the day of our full redemption is still in the future. Through Jesus' death and resurrection, God saved us from eternal separation, but we are still apart from him now. We still live on a planet that groans under the weight of sin (Rom. 8:22). Only in paradise will it be said, "No longer will there be any curse" (Rev. 22:3).

Eternally, he is good. And because he is good, he is trustworthy.

Clara, the little girl in *The Nutcracker*, trusted the dark and mysterious Herr Drosselmeier with her broken toy and her sadness. What seems like a paradox in the story describes God quite well. Even when we don't fully understand our mysterious Maker, we know he can *repair* our lives. We also know he cares for us because he is interested in our well-being.

King Solomon, known for his wealth and wisdom, was confident of this as he reflected over his life. He wrote, "I know that there is nothing better for men [and women] than to be happy and do good while they live. That everyone may eat and drink, and find satisfaction in all [their] toil—this is the gift of God. I know that everything God does will endure forever; nothing can be added to it and nothing taken from it . . ." (Eccles. 3:12–14). But Solomon also advised:

> When times are good, be happy;
>   but when times are bad, consider:
> God has made the one
>   as well as the other. . . .
>
>   Ecclesiastes 7:14

The residents of Lisbon, Portugal, found resolve with God also. Assuredly there was much pain and grief following their tragedy. Although nobody could replace what had been lost, the city rose again in beauty and grandeur. Like the early light that breaks through the blanket of night, they began to find shimmers of hope in their community and their faith.

"But as for me, I trust in you [God]." King David completes the writing of Psalm 55 with this solitary line addressed to God. He has moved through intense anguish, terror, and trembling into a path of hope that includes turning to God, communicating with God, and trusting in God. The journey of hope will be made complete for those who are led by the Spirit of God because we are children of God. We are not to be enslaved to fear but rather cry out, "*Abba,* Father!" (see Rom. 8:12–16).

What good is God when he doesn't provide safety from the storms? He is present with us. God is all-powerful, and his perfect love is as great as his power. His goodness encompasses the *eternal hope* he offers that supersedes the horror of our storms. Here we embrace newfound trust, the pillar of our peace in the midst of the storm.

3

If God Knows Everything, Why Doesn't He Do Something?

Doubt always coexists with faith, for in the presence of certainty who would need faith at all?

Philip Yancey

"Daddy, don't let go!" screamed my son Josh. "Daddy!"

I was running alongside him, holding the back of his bicycle. His eyes were wide with excitement and terror. "Daddy, don't leave me!" he yelled.

He began pedaling faster and faster, soon to outrun my aging legs. "You're doing great, Josh!" I assured. Neighbors had come outside to watch this climactic moment when a child finally rides his bike without training wheels. Scrambling beside him, I was no longer holding his bike. "Good job, Josh! Keep it up!" I panted as I began falling back.

Josh did marvelously! He rode perfectly straight and then began to turn in the cul-de-sac. As he began his turn, he glanced over his shoulder for the assurance that I was there. I wasn't.

Instead, I was thirty yards back panting and catching my breath. My smile should have been reassuring—but it wasn't.

"Daddy!" he yelled in panic. In a flash his handlebars twisted and he crashed hard to the pavement. I ran to him and picked him off of the bike. His crying soon stopped, followed by the accusations.

"I told you not to let go!" he demanded. "I'm never riding that bike again."

He didn't. Not without training wheels that is. It took me nearly a year to convince him that he was good enough to ride again without them.

Now here's a question. As a parent, I knew there was a very good chance Josh would crash. However, I let go. Why? If I knew this was about to happen, why didn't I do something to prevent it?

The answer would sound something like: We all grow and learn through the hard knocks of life—our crashes mature us. Sounds simple, doesn't it? However, simple only comes with simple territory. When we apply this question to God, it's complicated and full of mystery. Bruce and Jan's story, shared by Bruce's sister-in-law, sets the foundation for our question.

Ruler of All Nature

Bruce and Jan both worked at a Christian camp for three summers prior to their wedding. Their close friendship grew until they decided to get married. They were truly best friends first and foremost.

Jan's parents fell in love with Bruce and took him in as their own as they got to know him well. Bruce was a great guy—fun, athletic, hardworking—and he loved God and wanted to serve him as a missionary helicopter pilot. The family went to Jan's hometown the week before the wedding and had a wonderful time together.

Following an exquisite wedding, Bruce swept his bride off to their honeymoon in Costa Rica. On a scrumptious sun-filled Caribbean day, Bruce found a guy who loaned him a boogie board, and Bruce was having a blast in the surf. It was getting close to supper, and Jan, watching her new husband having so much fun, said that he should continue while she got ready for dinner.

Jan got ready and waited and waited and waited . . . then crazy thoughts started racing through her head as a small tropical storm quickly blew in. She changed clothes and ran out to the beach, which was by this time deserted except for a cluster of people down by the water. She ran over and, to her horror, saw a body with a sheet over it and a Costa Rican policeman speaking to a local.

Bruce had seen the storm approaching and decided to get out of the water and head back to their room. Walking along the beach with the boogie board underarm, he was struck by a lightning bolt and killed instantly.

In the months following his death, issues of safety and trust clutched at the throats of Bruce and Jan's families. Bruce's sister-in-law said to me, "I don't know how to pray for protection for my kids when I leave them. From whom do I ask protection? God himself?" We too struggle with such questions as, "Did God know this was about to happen?" If he called Bruce into ministry, did some "other" force overrule God and kill Bruce? If God allows evil, then by his choice of noninvolvement, he chooses not to help. Couldn't God have nudged the thunderbolt over a few feet to empty sand or a palm tree?

Some weeks later I was worshiping at my home church. We were singing choruses when an older hymn was introduced. The words were meant to be invigorating and inspiring, but as I sang the first stanza, Bruce and Jan's story flashed back into mind.

> Fairest Lord Jesus! Ruler of all nature!
> O Thou of God and man the Son!
> Thee will I cherish, Thee will I honor,
> Thou my soul's glory, joy, and crown![1]

I froze. *Ruler of all nature?* If this is true, then who was responsible for the fatal lightning bolt? Does God truly know everything? Why didn't he distract Bruce? Why didn't he do something?

Omniscience Is . . .

When I describe my children to people I meet, I describe them by their attributes. These are words describing a quality or their inherent characteristics. For example, my son Josh is creative and artistic. My daughter, Brianna, is dramatic, followed by her younger brother, the loud and boisterous Lucas. At first glance, these words can be confused with skills or abilities. But I'm using them to describe my children's inner nature. They have these qualities by nature and through the makeup of their character. As they age, these qualities will never change.

The same holds true in describing God. One of his attributes—an inherent characteristic that cannot be separated from his being—is his omniscience. Omniscient means "having infinite [absolutely without limit, endless] awareness, understanding, and insight."[2] Infinite awareness means nothing can ever "slip past God." God knows and sees everything. Infinite understanding, then, is God's unlimited comprehension. He truly knows and grasps all. God's infinite insight also brings into focus the truth that he intuitively sees the inner nature of things. That insight includes even the depths of our souls. Simply put, God knows.

God's infinite understanding can be misconstrued. Some stretch this attribute of God into such vagueness that his personhood is lost. Others claim that God's truth and comprehension are so far above ours that we can never catch a glimpse of God's truth. But this is contrary to what is written in the Bible. Instead, we can find the Bible to be our plumb line of truth given by God himself. The question is how do we relate at all to this omniscient mind? Scripture is necessary for us to relate to our infinite God. Panels of scholars contributing to the volumes of *Integrative Theology* offer this insight,

> As omniscient then, God's judgments are formed in the awareness of all the relevant data. God knows everything that bears upon the truth concerning any person or event.[3]

Beyond God's Mind, His Heart

In addition to knowing all the relevant data on any event, God always acts in harmony with his purposes of holy love. "We may not always be able to see that events in our lives work together for a wise purpose, but we know that God chooses from among all the possible alternatives the best ends and means for achieving them."[4]

In other words, God's infinite thought processes most certainly exceed our own. However, he has designed our minds in a way to comprehend him so that we can trust him. The purposes of God are good and loving, even when they make little sense to us due to *our* lack of relevant "data."

God most certainly knows all. He knew the lightning bolt would strike and kill Bruce. God is not limited in any way to what he can know. So we find ourselves back to our initial question: If God knows everything, why doesn't he do something?

"'For I know the plans I have for you,' declares the LORD, 'plans to prosper you and not to harm you, plans to give you hope and a future'" (Jer. 29:11). Those claiming blessing for their own often quote this Scripture. Did

> "God can permit evil only in so far as he is capable of transforming it into good."
>
> Augustine

you know, though, that God spoke this to Jeremiah amidst the great destruction of Jerusalem and the capture and exile of the nation's greatest leaders? Jeremiah has been named "the Weeping Prophet" precisely because of the calamity that destroyed his nation. God knows in advance the pain *and* has a plan for us. Even through the darkest times, God provides hope and a future.

God's infinite mind and purposes include a plan for you and me. My soul aches to know this plan because of the uncertainty of events lurking around tomorrow's corner. However, I must trust. My past has countless trophies of God's love in faith-shaping disasters and storms that changed me for the better.

Perhaps this is what Paul meant when he prayed for those Christians in Ephesus to "know this love [of God] that surpasses knowledge" (Eph. 3:19). Only by knowing the holy love of God will we experience that which surpasses all knowledge available to us mortals.

Pressing through Pain

Recently I underwent some serious pain. This pain was based in relationships gone sour, but it also had deep spiritual implications to it. I wept and prayed and found no reprieve for my anguish. I felt somewhat like the apostle Paul who cried out to God on three distinct occasions, "remove this thorn (this torment) from me!" And like God responded to Paul, God's reply to me also seemed like a resounding, "No."

These authors write words that express how my emotions run wild in times of distress:

> I feel loneliness, then fury. How can this happen? My fury glides into envy. Then I round the corner into stark, naked terror. All in the span of minutes, my emotions race like a wind through an open window, blowing every unfastened paper into a chaotic debris.[5]

How often does emotional pain drive us to settle for easy answers or to fill up our days just to escape the disquiet (all the voices running through our head)? Some of us can push back the noise during the day, but as the sun sets we are left only with dark silence, and our fears or insecurities come to haunt us again.

During this struggle that drew my soul very near dark depression, I purchased some exercise equipment for my basement. I began to work out every morning. During these workout sessions, what I learned about physical work and pain began shaping my thoughts on life and its struggles.

First, I discovered with a strange sense of crazy humor that I spent a lot of cash on equipment that hurt me! (It's amazing what we'll do to preserve our health.) I learned that every time I pressed against the weights, pain and exhaustion would fill my body. Still, I never quit. Pain, it seemed, was a valid part of this process. Pain was to be my partner and personal trainer. Without it I could never achieve my goals.

I also realized that once I mastered a certain level of physical struggle, I would experience a moment of exhilaration. Those moments were short-lived, however, because I would *increase* the weight. I never questioned that this behavior was correct in a weight room. Why? You know why.

The greater the opposition and energy expended, the greater the physical result. In a physical sense, I will grow stronger and healthier because of the continual increases causing pain. As my body ached and grew, my soul in this torn relationship also began to ache and grow. If I could look deep enough, I'm certain I'd find stretch marks clinging to my thoughts, maturity, and emotions. Fractured relationships continue, but my heart grows strong. The challenge is also to remain tender in heart, while emotional onslaught tempts me to rage in retaliation.

The Cry

When we feel out of control, we feel like we're not just lifting weights but like we're trapped beneath them. We feel alone without someone to "spot" us or help us lift a weight that is too much for us to handle. In those moments, we long to cry out for help.

Because of my ongoing intrigue and growing love of the ancient poetry written in the Psalms, I have marked certain passages that pull me through these moments of dread. I turn again to the words of Psalm 77:

> I cried out to God for help;
>   I cried out to God to hear me.
> When I was in distress, I sought the Lord;
>   at night I stretched out untiring hands
>   and my soul refused to be comforted.
> I remembered you, O God, and I groaned;
>   I mused, and my spirit grew faint.
>
>   verses 1–3

The psalmist sought the Lord. He mused and grew faint . . . and though he groaned, he hung in there. He didn't yell at his wife, grab a beer, then distract himself with a basketball game. He didn't go back to the office or make ten more phone calls. He remembered God. Although faint, he laid back down under the barbell of life and heaved again. The poet would not stop resisting against the weight of his agony until he received peace from God. *What do you want from me? I cannot survive unless I know something more about your purpose. What must I comprehend to understand you?*

After the death of his wife, C. S. Lewis wrote his reflections on grief in a profound work, *A Grief Observed*. Here he shares his private agony, "Do I hope that if *feeling* disguises itself as *thought* I shall feel less? Aren't all these notes the senseless writhings of a man who won't accept the fact that there is nothing we can do with suffering except to suffer it?"[6]

I believe Lewis came to realize that God did know everything. For him, the verb "to know" must have meant that God too had suffered through the pain Lewis was enduring.

There is a German word, *durchleiden*, for which there is no good English translation. It means to experience and get to know something by suffering. To "suffer a thing through" with your entire being, rather than trying to "figure it out."[7] What a great word! We can rationalize, theorize, philosophize, and debate until we die, but it is not until we "suffer a thing through" that we will "know." Though we must suffer through it, we don't suffer alone. We have God's omniscience—he knows our inmost thoughts and feelings. We are fully understood. We don't grieve alone. We are deeply known.

Stickability

The Bible was written by people who had to learn the powerful lessons of endurance and perseverance. They too had to grapple with emotional torments that challenged their confidence in God. One man in particular taught and spiritually guided the early followers of Jesus in the city of Jerusalem.

James had observed Jesus' life firsthand and knew the source of God's suffering and God's victory.

> Perseverance must finish its work so that you may be *mature and complete,* not lacking anything.
>
> James 1:4 (author's emphasis)

The fact that you are reading this page shows your desire to be fully alive (i.e., mature and complete—lacking nothing). Every being that breathes longs for a sense of completeness and maturity. But it doesn't come cheap. To live a full and complete life requires courage and determination—it doesn't just happen by default. We want to "arrive" in life. How does James, the writer of the passage above, suggest we get there?

Perseverance, the ability to keep on keeping on, must first finish its work for us. Ooh, doesn't sound like much fun. And I love to have fun! During those times in life when we experience extended times of pain or discomfort, it's easy to look for a way out.

> "Character is defined in life's uninspired moments."
>
> Author Unknown

Rev. Hal Noah, a pastor of a church where I interned in Dallas, once said, "The greatest ability you can have today is stickability." Too many people leave families, jobs, and churches on whims when the going gets tough. We need to learn to persevere. Another friend and mentor has challenged me repeatedly, "Doug, character is defined in life's uninspired moments." I agree! But it is in those uninspired moments or those times of extended pain that we yearn to bolt and run. Instead, God speaks to us through the author James and says, "Let perseverance complete its work in you." Don't run; endure.

Calvin Miller searched for timeless principles of spirituality in the classic writings of the saints in the Christian faith. He opens his book with this story:

> Scottish patriarchs, looking for walking sticks, always passed over the untried wood of the lower slopes. They climbed to the

wuthered heights to search for rods made strong by storm and wind. These iron-strong canes were once young trees that fought the icy Northers. With each storm they bent and twisted and broke a bit inside. But gradually each inner scar became the steely fiber they bought with every storm they endured.[8]

In order to be transformed, we need the pain or struggle. The breaking that occurs creates the "inner scars" that ultimately strengthen us. It's a prerequisite for those attaining maturity, completion, and the lack of nothing. That's why James told us to consider it pure *joy* when we endure trials of many kinds. When trials of various kinds explode your serene life, consider it a joy.

Now, joy seems like a bit of a stretch, but joy doesn't mean happiness here. It means being deeply affirmed in God's love for you. What affirmation it is to know that God has not found some escape hatch for us. Instead, in his infinite insight into our character, he believes in us. He knows we have the ability to endure. Our lives have significant purpose and meaning beyond this present moment.

The Quest for Spiritual Growth

To be successful requires a lot of hard work. In our studies, we set the bar of achievement high. (I've never purposefully crammed for an *F*.) Businesspeople know the challenges of achievement in our fields. As parents we've come to realize the obstacles that must be overcome in order to raise a family in this society. All these require diligent work in the face of struggle. In fact, they require hard work for a sustained period of time.

Why, then, do we question the character of God when we are not immediately rescued from struggle in our circumstances? We easily lose sight of spiritual wholeness or maturity, which promises delayed and intangible rewards. Spiritual hurdles such as patience, generosity, and gentleness often seem in direct opposition with our preset goals or our definitions of success.

Unlike the effects of a workout routine that can be measured for progress, we can't easily measure our spiritual gain. Rather than stepping on a scale or wrapping a measuring tape around our biceps, we measure spiritual gain by our affect on others. We must see through "spiritual eyes" to recognize how the struggle has strengthened us, encouraged others, and helped those we touch. Only then do we catch a glimpse of our true spiritual growth.

"In the Gray Zone"

I appreciate the writings of Rachel Naomi Remen, M.D., author of *My Grandfather's Blessings*. She is a woman who has not only practiced medicine, but has cared extensively for those with terminal illnesses. In a chapter titled "In the Gray Zone," Dr. Remen writes about the struggle of physicians to be in control of highly stressful and precarious situations.

> Perhaps the most basic skill of the physician is the ability to have comfort with uncertainty, to recognize with humility the uncertainty inherent in all situations. . . . The wish to control floats like a buoy above the hidden reef of fear. More than any single thing, fear is the stumbling block to life's agenda. . . . Life is process. When he was very old, Roberto Assagioli, the founder of psychosynthesis, reminded one of his young students of this: "There is no certainty; there is only adventure," he told this young man. "Even stars explode."[9]

To which I add, and God having infinite awareness, understanding, and insight, knows and sees all. Without control, we must trust in God.

The title of this book's first section, "What Good Is God in Life's Storms?" is a question based from this gray zone—from our inherent desire to be in control. When anguish arrives at the hands of another person, our defenses kick in and we adjust some part of that relationship to protect ourselves. That person was not safe and we must regain control. However, to turn our backs or to erect an emotional barrier between God and us when his control involves pain brings only damage rather than protection.

Rest for the Singer

The great psalmist, King David, often found himself in turmoil. Not only do his writings teach us how to worship and praise, but they also invite us to wrestle with doubt until it gives way to hope. They empower us to stay on a life path of change.

Psalm 62 records David's longing for a God of rest and refuge, similar to the hunchback yelling "Sanctuary!" in chapter 1. Throughout the ancient script, we read of David referring to God as his rock and fortress. He proclaims God as his source of rest and hope. We, like David, can discover the loving presence of God to be our source of strength. As we persevere in the grief following loss, or overwhelming fatigue after a bitter struggle, we can discover the supernatural strength that abides with us beyond reason and feeling. From there we can echo with David his analogy of God as our rock. God is truly unshakable. He is our impenetrable fortress in whom we find complete sanctuary.

Try a brief exercise with me. Recite David's poem below. Read it out loud. As you do, ask God to reveal his love to you. Spend a moment connecting with this all-loving, all-knowing God.

> My soul finds rest in God alone;
>   my salvation comes from him.
> He alone is my rock and my salvation;
>   he is my fortress, I will never be shaken.
> How long will you assault a man?
>   Would all of you throw him down—
>   this leaning wall, this tottering fence?
> They fully intend to topple him
>   from his lofty place;
>   they take delight in lies.
> With their mouths they bless,
>   but in their hearts they curse.
>   *Selah*

(pause for a moment here and ponder these things)

> Find rest, O my soul, in God alone;
>   my hope comes from him.
> He alone is my rock and my salvation;
>   he is my fortress, I will not be shaken.
> My salvation and my honor depend on God;
>   he is my mighty rock, my refuge.
> Trust in him at all times, O people;
>   pour out your hearts to him,
>   for God is our refuge.
>
>   *Selah*

(pause and reflect)

> Lowborn men are but a breath,
>   the highborn are but a lie;
> if weighed on a balance, they are nothing;
>   together they are only a breath.
> Do not trust in extortion
>   or take pride in stolen goods;
> though your riches increase,
>   do not set your heart on them.
> One thing God has spoken,
>   two things have I heard:
> that you, O God, are strong,
>   and that you, O Lord, are loving.
> Surely you will reward each person
>   according to what he has done.
>
>   Psalm 62

The Psalms are a mirror to the human soul. The psalmist's ruthless honesty compels us to look beyond the surface of our chaos. Perhaps if only for a moment you experienced the pulse of God's love and care for you, you too have caught a glimpse of his eternal purpose. When you read of his rest, did your heart ache or sigh? Reading that our salvation and honor depend on God can bring us to look deep within for the truth of our own existence.

There will be times when we wonder why God doesn't act. Our questions cause us to doubt his love and goodness, when in fact it may be our own limited sight that is at fault. Here we also discover the truth that Paul described: to trust or move toward this all-knowing God, we can only approach him through the embrace of his holy love. For only in that embrace can we know the love of God that surpasses knowledge. The final stanza of this psalm speaks only of strength and love. "You, O God, are strong and . . . you, O Lord, are loving" (Ps. 62:11–12).

The Mystery of God's Blessing

In 1991, I buried my infant daughter and young wife. I've wept and questioned and fought and turned from God. I've also experienced again his embrace in many ways, one of which is in the arms of an exquisite lady named Stephanie, my current wife. We now have two children from this marriage: Brianna and Lucas. With Josh, my son from Evon, my late wife, we make a family of five.

It is hard not to wonder why God didn't heal Evon. She had HIV, contracted from a simple blood transfusion. Our infant daughter Ashli contracted the same virus through birth. Did God know the virus was in that contaminated unit of blood? Yes. Did God have the power to avert the transfusion or even completely heal my wife and daughter from their infections? Most certainly. Then, if God knew all this, why didn't he do something?

I honestly don't know. But maybe, *just maybe* God knew personally a little girl and a little boy before they were formed in their mother's womb (see Jer. 1:5). It could be that the miracles I know as Bri and Luc were destined to come into being in my present family. Could it be that God wanted them to be born to Steph and myself? If the answer is "yes," then the painful deaths of Evon and Ashli had to occur first.

You see, this is what I call "the mystery of God's blessing." I don't understand it all. But I know that God loves me and his omniscient purposes supersede my ability to understand. God certainly could have healed my girls. He didn't. And at the time, it hurt immeasurably. My perspective today, though, has much more depth, length, and humble compassion. I'm still trying to absorb all the "relevant data" I can. I continually find myself dreadfully short in my understanding, while mysteriously blessed in life.

One God, One Love

For countless generations, Orthodox Jews have taught six Hebrew words, the *Sh'ma*, to children as soon as they are able to speak. Translated into English, they are: "Hear O Israel, the Lord God, the Lord is One." Traditionally the *Sh'ma* is said in times of great danger and at the moment of death. These words have always meant that despite suffering, loss, and disappointment, God can be trusted.[10]

What good is a God who knows everything but doesn't do something? He is good because he knows all and desires that we live a full life of deep joy. He has our greatest good in mind even when it includes great sorrow. Though we remain in the struggle and pain to mature and complete us, he knows our thoughts and our greatest fears. In his omniscience and his great love for us, he remains our fortress, our protection—our place of rest.

God is good as his purposes for us are good. "I know the plans I have for you," declares the Lord. If God seems to be sitting on his hands in your circumstance, don't turn away. Press in. Find him in the midst of your emotion. Engage again in the love that surpasses all understanding. Never give up. Trust in him at all times; pour your heart out to him.

Sometimes our prayer is as simple as this:

> *You, O God, are strong, and you, O Lord, are loving.*
> *Amen.*

4

Where Is God during the Blizzard?

If we postpone our journey till the storm dies down, we may never get started at all.

J. I. Packer

The waters were placid and warm. It was a beautiful sunny day at Aurora Reservoir as we strapped on our diving gear. This dive would complete our advanced certification for scuba diving. My dive buddy was the guy none of the women wanted to dive with. His loud comments in class frustrated us all. We clambered from shore, splashed into the lake, and swam out to the buoy.

Our instructor told us to go down to thirty feet and navigate a square at a minimum of twenty kicks per length. Once descended into the murky water, I confirmed with my buddy that we were set. Grabbing my compass, we set off.

At the second turn, something strange occurred. I turned ninety degrees to the right and swam directly into a whirlpool! A sudden rush of water spun me rapidly around and around.

I panicked and looked for my diving buddy, who was now out of sight. *He must have been swept away,* I thought. *Wait a second. A whirlpool? In a lake?* Trying desperately to get my direction as I spun violently counterclockwise, I suddenly glimpsed the fin of my partner. Up to my left and behind me, he too was evidently caught in the spin.

The cloudy water gave us a visibility of about five feet. I motioned to him. But as he descended toward me, I noticed he gave me an irritated look. *Come on, let's go,* he motioned. Then I realized what was happening.

You see, in scuba diving it is not uncommon to experience vertigo, a sensation in which you lose all sense of balance and direction. Because of a miscommunication between the inner ear and your eyes, it feels like you are spinning helplessly out of control.

I motioned to my buddy that I was experiencing vertigo. Impatient, he motioned for us to hurry up. He was unwilling to help me deal with the spinning sensation by holding onto me for a few moments to stabilize me. Instead I was forced to press on. Reaching for my compass again, I pointed it in the direction I thought we should be heading. Although I was still terrified and shaken, I forced the feeling aside to complete our maneuver.

Still "spinning," I began to swim. I felt the cramping in my rib cage as I struggled to stay on course. It seemed as if I had to continue to swim at a sharp right angle in order to keep the needle straight on the marker. We made our last turn and swam within six feet of our initial beginning point, having accomplished what was required for the skill test. We then ascended to the water's surface. What a relief it was to see the horizon again! As I saw the buoy marker, the vertigo decreased, and when my eyes viewed land, the vertigo stopped instantly.

Getting lost, whether in a lake or in life, is terrifying! When I was a child I visited my grandmother. Once while returning from the park near her house, I walked down a wrong street. I was so frightened when I "realized" someone had moved my grandma's house!

As adults, we still find ourselves grappling with the fear of being lost without any bearings or direction. Fear creates a sense of abandonment or deep loneliness. In the waters of Aurora Reservoir, I felt incredibly alone. Though my diving buddy was nearby, he was certainly no help. The sediment in the water seemed to spin around me, causing the perception that I was completely separated from my companion.

Sideways Snow

I experienced many blizzards growing up on a farm in Nebraska. Winters out on the plains bring phenomenal snowstorms that paralyze entire communities within minutes. If you've ever been caught out in a blizzard, you know well the dizzying isolation that accompanies a storm of this magnitude.

Funny how you don't see many Christmas postcards with blizzards or monsoons pictured on them! Instead, they display soft, fluffy white flakes resembling cutouts by children in warm schoolrooms. There is nothing peaceful about a blizzard. In high winds, pretty little snowflakes become icy daggers pummeling anything in their path. The storms come in lightning fast, and the snow blows in crazed directions. If you've ever driven in a snowstorm, you have found yourself staring at the countless thousands of white dots falling in front of your headlights. They then dance sideways before pirouetting up over the car hood, flirting at your window, and disappearing over you. At first beautiful, this orchestration becomes so repetitive that it leaves drivers hypnotic. Reality fuzzes, and it becomes very difficult to remain on the highway.

Schoolchildren's Blizzard

Few blizzards were so personally cruel and harrowing as the January 12 blizzard of 1888, known as the "School Children's Blizzard."[1] While other snowstorms brought greater amounts of snow or colder temperatures, this one combined gale winds, blinding snow, and rapidly falling temperatures, making it lethal.

The *Encyclopedia Britannica* of 1893 recorded the storm's power:

> In one [blizzard] which visited Dakota and the States of Montana, Minnesota, Nebraska, Kansas and Texas in January, 1888, the mercury fell within twenty-four hours from 74° above zero to 28° below it in some places, and in Dakota went down to 40° below zero. In fine clear weather, with little or no warning, the sky darkened and the air was filled with snow, or ice-dust, as fine as flour, driven before a wind so furious and roaring that men's voices were inaudible at a distance of six feet. Men in the fields and children on their way from school died ere they could reach shelter; some of them having been not frozen, but suffocated from the impossibility of breathing the blizzard. Some 235 persons lost their lives.

Because of the suddenness of this storm's onset, the blizzard caught many children away from home in their one-room schoolhouses of southeast Nebraska. O. W. Meier shared his experience; it's found in the Library of Congress's collection of life histories.

> At half past eight Walter, then 8, Henry, 12, and I, 15 years of age, started out thru the deep white snow. Pretty starry flakes made us look like snowmen before we reached the school, a mile and a half from home. Just when we got settled down to our books, the storm struck the north side of the house as swiftly as lightning. The whole building shivered and quaked. With a deafening whack the shutters were slammed shut by the terrific wind. In an instant the room became black as night, then for a moment there came a ray of light. I stood and said, "May my brothers and I go home?" The teacher said, "Those boys who live south may put on their coats and go, but the rest of you must stay here in this house."

Nearby, Eva Thieves's husband saw how cold it was going to be, and he started from the hotel on a boardwalk and crawled on his hands and knees to another schoolhouse where he knew that the teacher and eight children could not get out of the school. He then followed the boardwalk to keep track of the edge of the walk and brought back the teacher and children and kept them there until the next day at his hotel.[2]

Meanwhile, the Meier brothers had entered the wintry blast.

We had not gone a rod when we found ourselves in a heap, in a heavy drift of snow. We took hold of each other's hands, pulled ourselves out, got into the road, and the cold north wind blew us down the road a half mile south, where the Strelow boys and John Conrad had to go west a mile or more.

My brothers and I could not walk thru the deep snow in the road, so we took down the rows of corn stalks to keep from losing ourselves 'till we reached our pasture fence. Walter was too short to wade the deep snow in the field, so Henry and I dragged him over the top. For nearly a mile we followed the fence 'till we reached the corral and pens.

The roaring wind and stifling snow blinded us so that we had to feel thru the yard to the door of our house. Pa had gone out to meet us but was forced back by the storm. We stayed in the house all that night. It was so cold that many people froze to death in the snow.

"That was an awful night on the open plains," recalls O. W. Meier. "Many teachers and school children lost their lives in that blinding storm, while trying to find their way home. The blizzard of 1888 has not been forgotten."[3]

～

Our question for this chapter asks, "Where is God during the blizzard?" It matters little whether the blizzard ravaged settlers of 1888 or knocks out power and scrambles technology today. Regardless of the development of civilization and technology, the forces of nature bring humanity to its knees, pleading for mercy from the God of the storm.

Storms of the Heart

Have you ever been in a blizzard? This time I'm not talking about the snowy kind. Has your life been wonderful, then a storm hits? Gale winds hammer against all that you considered secure, forcing you to cling to any stable thing you can find in life. In this storm you find the onslaught intense and disorienting. You have trouble knowing "which way is up" and you feel, in a strange sense, all alone. As you try to make sense of the chaos, the details and fragments of pain blast like sideways snow, leaving you numb.

There are many kinds of blizzards: relational, spiritual, financial, physical. These howling, swirling storms leave us vulnerable, threatening to make us lose our way. Our heartfelt plea is for assurance that there is an order of reality that far transcends our problems. *Somehow,* we whisper nervously to ourselves, *everything is going to be okay*. Joni Eareckson Tada describes,

> We amble on along our philosophical path then—Bam!—get hit with suffering. No longer is our fundamental view of life providing a sense of meaning or a sense of security in our world. Suffering has not only rocked the boat, it's capsized it. We need assurance that the world is not splitting apart at the seams. We need to know we aren't going to fizzle into a zillion atomic particles and go spinning off in space. We need to be reassured that the world, the universe, is not in nightmarish chaos, but orderly and stable. God must be at the center of things. He must be in the center of our suffering.[4]

In the center of our suffering or darkness, then we look to him. But again all we see is blackness. We crazily long to believe in God, but we only see the dark world and evil laced with suffering.

Part of the mystery of God is his intrusion, which provides us with what we desperately desire, not what we think we require. He does so by the use of paradox: He draws us to darkness and, in the midst of what appears awful, God shows us something of his awe-full, bright goodness.

"A philosopher once asked, 'Where is God?'

The Christian answered, 'Let me first ask you, where is he not?'"

John Arrowsmith

As the Great Ruler, we wonder about the boundaries to God's kingdom. Does he rule over storms, or has he relinquished control of the earth's dynamic to another cosmic or demonic force? Maybe the laws of nature are set by him, and he refuses to touch the order. I find it is easier to accept a God that rules in only spiritual dimensions. He certainly is known as the Prince of Peace. It only makes sense, though, that if God is Lord over all that is created as well as the spiritual world, then he too by inclusion must be ruler over the darkness.

God of the Dark

> The LORD is my light and my salvation—
> Whom shall I fear?
>
> Psalm 27:1

When masses of people endure a similar agony as we do, we gain some comfort knowing that our story is not utterly unique. Yet, there are points in life that our journey is a private one. Our search for the face of God is done alone. Even when people are within our reach, we are forced to walk through the debris seeking truth.

We study God to learn his heart, his system, and hopefully to get a glimpse of his purpose. If he created this world, it only makes sense to better know him to best navigate his domain. J. I. Packer, renowned for his book *Knowing God,* describes it this way.

> As it would be cruel to an Amazonian tribesman to fly him to London, put him down without explanation in Trafalgar Square and leave him, as one who knew nothing of English or England, to fend for himself, so we are cruel to ourselves if we try to live in this world without knowing about God whose world it is and who runs it. The world becomes a strange, mad, painful place, and life in it disappointing and unpleasant business, for those who do not know about God.[5]

And for those who do not know about God, the path is painted with the blackest pitch. Maybe this is why I am a light addict. Lights seem to indicate life to me. Someone is home. We journey spiritually, looking for some type of light. It seems we long for someone to take residence and be "home" deep within our soul. As some try harder and harder to enlighten themselves, however, they find their own "light" adding to the chilling mix. There must be a way through these storms without freezing alone in close proximity to a friend. Friend, there is a way!

> "God is above, presiding; beneath, sustaining; within, filling."
>
> Hildebert of Lavardin

The light at the end of the tunnel is not a train. We must have faith that in this darkness there is a God. Scripture states that faith is the "substance of things hoped for" (Heb. 11:1). But "hope that is seen is no hope at all," Paul told the Romans (Rom. 8:24). He mentions some of the good things that might come out of difficulties: "Suffering produces perseverance; perseverance, character; character, hope" (Rom. 5:4). He lists hope at the end, instead of where I would normally expect it, at the beginning, as the fuel that keeps a person going. No, hope emerges from the struggle.

Our struggle in the darkness begins and ends with an emergence of hope. God is God even of the darkest minute.

Lord of the Storm

> The LORD is the stronghold of my life—
> of whom shall I be afraid?
>
> Psalm 27:1

The blinding life-storm makes us feel dizzy or mesmerized. We could easily be frozen or immobilized by pondering, "Was I in the wrong place at the right time?" Though you took all precautions you could foresee, the situation you find yourself in now is unexpected and holds you hostage.

We must not freeze in panic or dread. Instead we must keep moving, taking small steps to safety. While trying to find the way out of our dangerous situation, we must stay alert. We remain sharp to the details around us—landmarks that set our path. Our spirits must awaken to the presence of God.

How do we know when it's God? It is easy to lose our way in this complex, secular world. The journey is daunting, and our steps are often dogged by false turns and disaster. We must keep moving, but it is an act of dependence on our guide. And God has not left us stranded. We have a compass, a boardwalk, a cornrow to follow.

The compass in our hands is God's Word to us. Most important is his instruction in the Bible, but he speaks through his people as well. Many works, both ancient and contemporary, were written by those who heard God's direction. Listen to his voice and let it guide you.

We are compelled to trust and obey him. Though vertigo caused me to feel like I was swimming at a sharp angle in the reservoir, the compass indicated otherwise. Everything in me screamed, "No! You're going the wrong way. You'll swim in a circle!" But I forced myself to ignore those feelings. I followed the direction of the arrow on my compass and found my destination.

While the chaos of circumstances can be disorienting, this spiritual vertigo calms once the focus is set on the Lord of the storm. Scripture echoes his stability as ancient authors ascribe him as "the Rock of our salvation."

The psalmist doesn't reflect on snowstorms, but he does use a similar metaphor of a storm-tossed vessel in the open sea. Here is an ancient version of sailors who lost their sea legs.

> Others went out on the sea in ships;
>   they were merchants on the mighty waters.
> They saw the works of the Lord,
>   his wonderful deeds in the deep.
> For he spoke and stirred up a tempest
>   that lifted high the waves.

> They mounted up to the heavens and went down to the
>   depths;
>   in their peril their courage melted away.
> They reeled and staggered like drunken men;
>   they were at their wits' end.

Psalm 107:23–27

Do you see the similarities of the storms? These men enjoyed the beauty of nature and the weather. Then a storm blew in that lifted them to the heavens and down to the depths. Each wave caused them to ride out of control in the mighty surge. As in the blizzards of the plains, all the qualities of man failed and "melted away." Dizzied and irrational, they were like drunken men who stagger and are lost.

God in the Boat

Even weathered fishermen handpicked by Jesus himself found themselves in such a storm. The unique twist in this story is that Jesus is with them but fast asleep in the helm of their boat. Matthew briefly records that the disciples went to Jesus and awoke him with panicked voices. "Lord, save us! We're going to drown!" (Matt. 8:25). For experienced seamen to talk this way, it must have been quite a storm! Jesus' reply dealt with their faith first; then he calmed the storm by a vocal command. Stunned, they looked at one another and whispered, "Who is this, that even the winds and waves obey him?"

Later in his writings, Matthew told another story involving a storm at night. As these men were rowing against a great wind and the waves, they saw Jesus walking on the lake! Thinking they saw a ghost, they again cried out in fear. Jesus immediately calmed them by saying, "Take courage! It is I. Don't be afraid" (Matt. 14:27). Peter challenged and said, "Lord, if it's you, tell me to come to you on the water." Jesus saw Peter's faith and called him out. Miraculously, Peter also began walking on the water. But when he considered the stormy blast and took his eyes off Jesus, he began to "melt away" and sink. Quickly, Jesus reached out his hand and caught his friend, saying, "You of little faith, why did you doubt?"

In two storms we find Jesus. In the psalmist's storm, we find a God who hears and answers. Have you ever wondered where God *is* in the storms?

Prince of Peace

The psalmist continues his song about the storm-tossed sea and the sailors imprisoned within the waves.

> Then they cried out to the LORD in their trouble,
>   and he brought them out of their distress.
> He stilled the storm to a whisper;
>   the waves of the sea were hushed.
> They were glad when it grew calm,
>   and he guided them to their desired haven.
> Let them give thanks to the LORD for his unfailing love
>   and his wonderful deeds for men.
> Let them exalt him in the assembly of the people
>   and praise him in the council of the elders.
>
> Psalm 107:28–32

In his commentary on the Psalms, Derek Kidner suggests that this psalm "speaks not of our guilt but of our littleness. The hurricane shakes us into seeing that in a world of gigantic forces we live by permission, not by good management."[6] We most certainly agree! Who can tame the ocean's hurricane or the plain's blizzard? No human can.

Where Is God in the Blizzard?

As the Meier brothers braved the blizzard of 1888, God walked with them. The sailors in the psalmist's metaphor found a God who stood near the mast when they cried out to him.

Even the disciples of Jesus discovered a God who would come to earth in the form of man and abide with us in our storms.

God has never been "outside" the storm watching you fight it. No, he has always been at its center with you. His presence envelops you as the waves threaten. His warm breath can be sensed deep within as you trudge on in the freezing white.

In times of crises our beliefs will be shaken. Our faith, family values, and even loyalty is tested. Trusted parents and ministers are questioned. Religious experiences, sentimentality, and hype all blow away. Even God's presence is hard to feel. Was it all an illusion?

> "You need not cry very loud; he is nearer to us than we think."
>
> Brother Lawrence

In the blizzard, you may have to look at the fence line or the weeds along the road to find your way home. God has provided a path for you. In active faith, trust that it leads out of the storm. Amidst the journey, grasp the hope that God is there.

When the storm's nauseating highs and lows tempt you to lose all hope and courage, call out to the Almighty. The Prince of Peace alone can calm the waters. He is with you. You are never alone.

Where is God in the blizzard?

He's right beside you.

A Prayer to the God of Ebb and Flow

Dear Lord, today I thought of the words of Vincent Van Gogh: "It is true there is an ebb and flow, but the sea remains the sea." You are the sea. Although I experience many ups and downs in my emotions and often feel great shifts and changes in my inner life, you remain the same. Your sameness is not the sameness of a rock, but the sameness of a faithful lover. Out of your love I came to life; by your love I am sustained; and to your love I am always called back. There are days of sadness and days of joy; there are feelings of guilt and feelings of gratitude; there are moments of failure and moments of success; but all of them are embraced by your unwavering love.

My only real temptation is to doubt in your love, to think of myself as beyond the reach of your love, to remove myself from the healing radiance of your love. To do these things is to move into the darkness of despair.

O Lord, sea of love and goodness, let me not fear too much the storms and winds of my daily life, and let me know that there is ebb and flow but that the sea remains the sea.
Amen.[7]

5

How Can People Speak of Joy?

Spare me the theology; just give me the story.

Tim Winton, Australian novelist

Eva was a great host and marvelous cook. We sat across from each other, and she shared how she and her husband had met. Of course she was trying to embarrass him, and judging by his blushed cheeks she was successful. Her love for life and a good laugh made eating a challenge. There were times when we laughed so hard, I was afraid I'd launch some of my pasta! After dinner we sat comfortably in the living room and talked about life and God. The subject of the afterlife and eternity came up often, and we all shared deeply.

As we got into the car to go home, I commented to my wife how wonderful that couple was. She agreed, noting that they were especially fun to be around even though Eva was dying of cancer. I nodded in agreement and drove on.

Although I am intimately aware of the dynamics of their situation, I still ponder how some people can emit such joy in the midst of trying times. It intrigued me then and still does today.

At another encounter, I spent an extended lunch with a gifted man who had endured a tragic loss of a child. I found him to be different. In fact, it seemed to me that there was such heaviness over him that it made it difficult to spend much time with him.

Both experiences were shared with people undergoing great pain. However, one person breathed joy and strength into me while the other *drew* life and energy from me. This difference is worth some discussion and thought. When I leave people, I want to know that their joy overflows on account of my being with them. Rather than a dank experience, it's my desire to be a fresh breeze in their day. Can we speak of joy in the midst of someone's pain?

> "How far the story matters to anyone but myself depends on the degree to which others have experienced what I call 'joy.'"
>
> C. S. Lewis

How Can They Speak of Joy?

At a Village Inn, I sat numb after the funeral of my infant daughter. While sitting there, I slowly became aware of the atmosphere in the restaurant. The clanking of dishes and metal ringing of silverware was laced with the sounds of conversation and laughter. Like popcorn erupting in a hot kettle, conversations burst into laughter across the room. Typically laughter breeds laughter. For me that day, it birthed anger. Laughter seemed ludicrous and obscene against the backdrop of my intense grief.

How can they be so happy? I fumed. Everyone in the restaurant seemed oblivious to the shroud of darkness that cloaked my world that day. *Don't they realize how close each of us lives to death?*

Tragic moments often cause us to wonder how life was once glorious. Lying on my deck the day my brother was removed from life support, I looked into beautiful blue skies dotted with puffy, white clouds. *Black,* I murmured to myself. *The sky should be black.*

When you find yourself in a valley dark with shadows, everything looks black for a time. Walking friends down the valley of grief or suffering isn't easy either. Not only is it often terrifying, it can, in fact, sometimes be frustrating. Deep inside, we want them better. Pushing them through the process only causes additional pain, however.

Whether suffering through our own tragedies or walking with others in times of great distress, we would certainly never think of these moments as happy. Yet it is possible to experience joy even in dark times. Giants of the faith would agree. In the annals of history and Scripture, they described knowing joy in the wake of uncertainty, famines, battles, exiles, and even torture. I marvel at the trials previous civilizations have endured. Those who have gone before us bring us courage that we too can find this joy and hope that endures in spite of present circumstances.

What Joy Is Not

Children are the most whimsical little creatures around. Their personalities are dynamic and their emotions can be so extreme. They can move from happiness to anger and then to sadness and back to happiness in a matter of minutes. (Seven minutes to be exact. I just timed my children playing outside my office door.)

Though we love seeing our children happy, we know that in approximately seven minutes, they will experience frustration, anger, sadness, elation, and—if we're lucky and their diapers are dry, their tummies are full, and if they've had their naps— happiness again.

Happiness is a wonderful emotion. However, it is just that— an emotion. Emotion links our internal and external worlds. So, being aware of what we feel can open us to questions that are sometimes more easily ignored. Emotions are like the wind— full of mystery. They come and go suddenly, often leaving havoc and debris in their wake. This is why counselors spend many hours working with clients to direct these powerful forces in our lives.[1]

We spend a great deal of energy trying to ride on the crest of happiness. When there, we sail fast and free. When it ebbs, we fight a powerful undertow that threatens to wash us out. Many people spend much of their lives trying to "hang ten" with activities, parties, and hobbies that provide a constant emotional buzz. These aren't bad in themselves, but we've all met people who seem to live from one wave to the next. Whatever it takes to keep feeling happy is the main focus of their existence.

At the opposite end of the continuum are those who refuse to place any hope or expectations on happiness whatsoever. Instead, they climb into their cave of isolation or depression. Like emotional hermits, these people know how fleeting happiness can be and they skip the roller-coaster effect by avoiding the feeling completely. These people have crossed our paths too, and though we long to see them laugh and experience life with a smile, they exhaust our efforts with skilled ease.

> "If you have no joy in your religion, there's a leak in your Christianity somewhere."
>
> Billy Sunday

There is nothing wrong with being happy. If, however, our lives are filled with frantic chasing after happiness, an alarm should sound deep within that we need a stable spiritual source. In comparison to fleeting drops of happiness in the scorching heat, joy is a cool spring offering water where we can kneel and drink deeply.

What Joy Is

How do we know which is which? The difference between happiness and joy is as broad as it is deep. You see, happiness bases its source on what is happening. Good happenings result in feelings of happiness. *Something else* must then be the source of joy.

Open the page with me to a story set in Egypt with the ancient Hebrew people called the Israelites. If you have ever watched

Charlton Heston playing Moses as he leads the nation of Israel out of bondage, you can visualize the desert that serves as the backdrop of this story. The Israelites were under Egyptian control as slaves, being severely mistreated, when Moses arrived on the scene to lead his people out of bondage.

As the children of Israel left Egypt, the Book of Exodus describes how they "did as Moses instructed and asked the Egyptians for articles of silver and gold and for clothing. The LORD had made the Egyptians favorably disposed toward the people, and they gave them what they asked for; so they plundered the Egyptians" (Exod. 12:35–36).

They soon ventured into the desert following their great leader, Moses. They had wealth from Egypt and fresh clothing. As they experienced the many trials of the desert, God led them and supernaturally worked miracle after miracle. Imagine! They were not only protected and guided by God, but they had all the possessions they needed, and miracles became as ordinary as the sunrise!

No longer slaves, their whole future and the Promised Land stretched out before them. The Israelites had happiness written all over the pages of history that day.

As we know, happiness soon fades and it faded for Israel. They had the man, the money, and the miracles. But they soon began grumbling and complaining. Even the patience of God was put to the test, and the Bible says God became irritated with their attitudes. Consequently, God led his people in circles through the desert for forty years. Moses and his people had many lessons to learn, and though they had times of celebration and moments of gratitude, they will forever be remembered for their grumbling.

Speed forward with me hundreds of years through history, past the arrival of the Israelites to the Promised Land, past the vast empire of King David and the wealth of the nation under his son, Solomon. Let's look now at the nation Israel in 605 B.C. As a result of turning their hearts away from God, they found themselves in bondage again, only this time they were enslaved to the nation of Babylon. Their choice leaders had been taken captive into another country, and the precious land God had given them now lay in waste. The temple built by King Solomon—once a marvel to kings and kingdoms of that day—sat in ruins. The wall around their capital city was a crumbled mess. Listen to Psalm 137, written while the Israelites were in captivity in Babylon.

> By the rivers of Babylon we sat and wept
>   when we remembered Zion.
> There on the poplars
>   we hung our harps,
> for there our captors asked us for songs,
>   our tormentors demanded songs of joy;
>   they said, "Sing us one of the songs of Zion!"
> How can we sing the songs of the LORD
>   while in a foreign land?
> If I forget you, O Jerusalem,
>   may my right hand forget its skill.
> May my tongue cling to the roof of my mouth
>   if I do not remember you,
>   if I do not consider Jerusalem
>   my highest joy.
>
> verses 1–6

Can you imagine the pain in their hearts while they mourned the loss of their temple and holy city? Anger and despair rose within them as their captors tormented and mocked them, demanding songs of joy. They were a broken and lost nation without recourse. They were estranged from the presence of God. They looked to him for a rescue amidst the torments of their captors. Once, the temple of Zion had echoed with great songs of praise to the Creator. Now their harps hung silent, swinging from branches in the hot foreign winds.

Before we move on to what changed the Israelites, I must ask this, "Are the songs you once sang echoing only in the caverns of your memory? Have you hung your harps of gladness on the branches of weeping willow trees in a foreign land of despair?" If so, I have good news. You are in a place where God can bring about change. Watch how he does so with his chosen nation!

Time passed and the temple of Jerusalem lay in ruins. Again the nation of Israel cried out to God for deliverance. No Moses to arrive on the scene. This time, God used different people to guide his people. Through the efforts of a cupbearer to the king and a handful of prophets, God brought about their release.

They didn't have a great leader like Moses to direct them home. Nor did they have the wealth of their captors. Astonishing miracles did not await them either. What awaited them this time? Shambles.

With bags of seed rice to plant crops, the children of Israel walked in the rags of their captivity back to Jerusalem. The camera of my mind pans across the landscape behind their caravans. I see slumped and ragged shoulders of exhausted people. Hands blackened and wrinkled by the sun grasp walking sticks. Determination and hope presses them on. As they arrive at the edge of the rubble covering the foundation of their great temple, only then do they lay down their bags of precious rice. As the camera moves at a sharp angle to show their faces, I anticipate great sadness in their eyes. But what a shock! Read how one psalmist describes the Israelites' arrival back into Jerusalem or Zion—their dream of a perfect homeland.

> When the LORD brought back the captives to Zion,
>   we were like men who dreamed.
> Our mouths were filled with laughter,
>   our tongues with songs of joy.
> Then it was said among the nations,
>   "The LORD has done great things for them."
> The LORD has done great things for us,
>   and we are filled with joy.
> Restore our fortunes, O LORD,
>   like streams in the Negev.
> Those who sow in tears
>   will reap with songs of joy.
> He who goes out weeping,
>   carrying seed to sow,
> will return with songs of joy,
>   carrying sheaves with him.

Psalm 126

Can you see the tears streaming down over their quivering smiles? They were a nation that was completely broken. They had hit bottom and had nothing left, except some rice seeds, salty tears, and newfound joy. Through their tears they looked to their true source and gave him praise. They were "filled with joy."

Were they happy? Absolutely! Were they joyous? Of course! Happiness would soon fade as they walked from the temple ruins to rebuild their homes; but the joy wouldn't. Though we may experience joy and happiness simultaneously, they are independent of each other. I imagine hope in their eyes as they swept clean the crumbled foundations and carried wood to reframe entrances for their simple homes. The Israelites knew firsthand that, "Joy is the lasting sum reality of all our life experiences. It envelops both suffering and celebration."[2]

> "Joy is peace dancing and peace is joy at rest."
>
> F. B. Meyer

In contrast to the grumbling nation led by Moses, these Israelites coming out of Babylonian exile found a source of joy. This mystery of God abides much deeper than any man-made happiness. Its home is deeper than the pain and agony we may feel. True joy is a fruit of our spirit that is always in season when our hearts are connected with the heart of the Creator.

L'Chaim! a single Hebrew word that means "To life!" is always said with great enthusiasm as a toast in Jewish homes. It means that no matter what difficulty life brings, no matter how hard or painful or unfair life is, life is holy and worthy of celebration. It is believed that the sweetness of the wine reminds us that life itself is a blessing.

Unlike our American "Cheers!" toast, *L'Chaim!* is not a toast to happiness. Rather, a people who have lost and suffered have offered it down through the generations and truly understand that life is sacred and filled to the brim with lasting joy.[3]

You see, joy grows from within. Happiness comes from without. As our soul connects with the Spirit of the Creator, there is a wonderful upsurge from within us! Peace abides with and blankets our being. Love envelops us and moves us forward in compassion. Hope raises our eyes to focus on the truth of our future. Then there is joy, that source of energy that causes people to wonder why we can be in such dire circumstances and yet be content.

How Can I Find Joy?

There are indeed times, as Frederick Buechner says, that we may be surprised or delighted by joy. There are also times when we must sort through our emotions in order to have the capacity to receive joy. And there are also times when we must confess God's lordship over the fickle circumstances of life. This is a pouring out of our self-pride. Once empty, we are then ready to be filled with something more than ourselves.

Having gone through dark valleys of my own, I have screamed my questions to the heavens. I have also been surprised and delighted by joy from deep within. In fact, a strange phenomenon now occurs. When I meet people, I can tell who has had similar experiences in the dark times. Moreover, I can sense who has come through it and found joy as their source of strength. These people have what I call the "fragrance of the fire."

Don't you love singing around a bonfire, roasting marshmallows and getting away with novice pyro-tricks? Who can forget climbing into the car for the ride home only to discover that your fingers stick together in funny places from making s'mores, and your clothes and hair retain that unmistakable bonfire aroma from the smoke you choked on when the wind shifted? When a person has endured fiery trials of various kinds, they too have a distinct "aroma"—the fragrance of the fire. Instantly they gain my respect. Those who have the fragrance have found joy to be their source of strength.

In the opening story of this chapter, I shared of a couple whose wife was dying of cancer. She did eventually pass away. But her joy never did. People crowded the church building for her funeral. We hurt for our loss of a dear friend. I can tell you, though, we all left strengthened by her joy. We too want to emanate joy as she did in life. She inspired us.

What good is God when we find ourselves in despair while people speak of joy? He offers us the source of true joy in our souls. Unlike man-made happiness, joy is a mystery of God. As we come to the end of our sowing in tears, we will find that God's goodness conquers again. He brings a new joy that supersedes our circumstances. The nation of Israel reminds us of the paradox of celebration and suffering. Frederick Buechner said it best, "Where you have known joy, you have known God."[4] Memories of God's divine love for his people encourage us to believe again.

> "Joy is indeed the most infallible proof that his [God's] indwelling Spirit is in us: God is in his heaven and all's right with our lives and our world."
>
> Calvin Miller

Memory fastens down our thinking. We ask you to remember the goodness and faithfulness of a God who loves us. Isn't it strange how we long for longevity and history—yet we are unwilling to discipline our thinking or our traditions to hold our thoughts captive to the real and pure things of God. How quickly we are swept away by cultural norms, present concerns, or worries about tomorrow. So I ask you to remember:

Remember how the Israelites were set free. Remember how they entered into a broken land of burned-out houses. Remember, how the psalmist said they carried little bags of seeds and they planted the seeds in the scorched earth, crying over the desolation of their war-torn farms; then came the rain and the sun and the faithfulness of God. Then came the harvest—sheaves of grain, and bread, and laughter.[5]

L'Chaim! To life!

Almighty God,
Grant that we may never be entirely content with whatever bounty the world may bestow upon us, but that we may know at last that we were created not for happiness but for joy, and that joy is to the one alone who, sometimes with tears, commits his or her heart in love to you and to one another. Amen.[6]

Part 2

What Good Is God in Life's Tragedies?

The angst expressed in story after story of section 1, What Good Is God in the Storms? found us asking hard theological questions in the midst of tragedies of natural disasters and catastrophes delivered under God's control. These "acts of God," as we call them, have no one to blame as the cause. The pain we experience comes from a source beyond human control.

Section 2 moves us into a new area. When someone else makes a choice that deeply hurts us, we often wonder of God's goodness there. This is the next part of our journey with its companion question: What good is God in life's tragedies?

As I was completing this manuscript, I awoke to the horror of the terrorist attack on American civilians on September 11. My bags were packed for the airport for a speaking engagement, but instead I sat home and watched the events unravel all day. My heart broke and I continue to weep for those impacted—many of you reading these pages. Throughout the travesty, I heard the question again in my soul: What good is God in this tragedy?

God certainly knew of the planned attacks and hijackings. He was not without power to intervene or at least inform someone to do so. Yet I watched the collapse of the World Trade Center towers and continued to hear gripping stories of those innocent victims. My heart begins to shift the anger and blame from God to the dirty hands of those who orchestrated such evil.

These "faceless cowards" as President George W. Bush aptly described them are the sources of the attack on our beloved nation. It is easy to burn in hatred and revenge toward them.

Yet while we can focus our vengeance upon the humans who caused our pain, we still struggle with our question: What good is God in life's tragedies? As we continue our journey—hearts torn afresh—may God reveal his goodness even in the heat of our questions.

6

Does God Feel
This Ache You Carry?

Be kind, for everyone you meet is fighting a great battle.

Philo of Alexandria

Tears streamed down her face. She was wringing her hands as she shared the story of her daughter's death in a traffic accident. This middle-aged mom shared how a hurried taxi driver flew down the highway and sideswiped their van. Her nine-year-old daughter was launched through the large side window onto the highway in western Colorado. The mother pulled herself from the tangled wreck and ran to her daughter. With her head in her mother's lap, the girl died there on the highway. All I could do was cry with the mother and let her share her pain with me.

As I wait with those in excruciating pain, I feel waves of help-lessness wash over me. I sit with this grieving mother and long to absorb her pain like a giant sponge. If I could just turn the clock back, I would; if I had any power at all, I would bring her daughter back. But I am left only to engage in her agony for brief moments at a time. Though I may stay with her for an entire day and night or walk beside a family for several months, their pain far outlasts my ability to bear such burdens. No human heart can fully bear the burdens of pain and grief the world heaps on those around them.

Today, our nation weeps in remembrance of the terrorism in New York and Washington, D.C. As hard as I try, I cannot remove the pictures, both real and imagined, of innocent faces seconds before fatal impact. Something deep within me stirs.

I pause again and I hear another question. It pulls for my complete attention. I cry out, *"God, do you feel this ache?"* If so, I wonder if he even cares. How much does this suffering woman or a bruised nation matter to him?

The Face of God

I love looking deep into the windows of a person's soul, the eyes. Life can be intoxicating while watching the delight of a child, the adoration of a grandparent, or the expression of a student when a concept comes together and he "gets it."

Long solitary hours of writing are hard on me if I don't get the opportunity to interact daily with people face-to-face. I love to listen, but there are times when I need to talk. These are times of distress or intense emotion, times when my burden can only be released by the encouraging expression of a friend.

When we carry burdens so heavy that another human cannot help us, when we have nowhere else to turn, we search for God. We yearn for a God who has expressions of warmth and tangible concern. In times of great urgency or remorse we don't want to cry out to the air wondering if God is somewhere in it. We want a face.

Does God Feel This?

The cruelty of death becomes a stark reality when a warm body that can be held becomes a cold, intangible shell. Intimacy disappears, leaving only grief in its void. In *A Grief Observed,*

C. S. Lewis pondered the reality and finality of death. Lewis describes aspects of living after the loss of a dear one. He never anticipated the anguish of losing the memory of his wife's facial features and expressions. "Kind people have said to me, 'She is with God.' In one sense that is most certain. She is now, like God, incomprehensible and unimaginable."[1]

Is this all we get? A God who is incomprehensible and unimaginable? If so, how can God possibly feel the remorse and agony of his creation? For many the face of God remains a mystery.

Bibles and Crosses

> "The face is the mirror of the mind; and eyes, without speaking, confess the secrets of the heart."
>
> Saint Jerome

I was still in college when we discovered my late wife's HIV infection. Needless to say, my faith was deeply shaken. During that semester I was taking a homiletics (preaching) class with Dr. Jimmie Brewer. He had no idea of our situation.

Entering his office one afternoon, I slumped down in a chair across from Dr. Brewer's desk. "What's wrong, Doug?" he asked. I slid my Bible across his desk to him. "Prove to me that God is real," I said numbly. He paused for quite some time and never looked at the book. Instead, he studied my face. Then he gently leaned forward and slid the Bible back to me. "Prove it yourself," he replied. Although it felt harsh at the moment, it was one of the best pieces of advice I've ever received.

My question really was, "How can I engage with God's promises if I'm not sure he's engaged with my reality today?" Many of us have found the flannel graph image of the Sunday school Jesus sufficient until a crisis comes our way. "Is God real?" "Prove it yourself," he said. Any other answer to a question like mine would damage our relationship with God. This "proving" often requires a journey into what Saint John of the Cross describes as "the Dark Night of the Soul." Only through this wrestling with God, however, can we ever find the ownership of both our pain and our resolve.

Those of us who grew up in the Protestant tradition learned early never to make a graven image of Christ. We do not have icons or statues that might tempt us to worship something other than the unseen God. We have been taught that we cannot look upon the face of God because we would be blinded by his glory. In his awesome presence we fall prostrate before him. This is undoubtedly true, but could it be equally true that we cannot possibly bear to look upon the immense suffering in the face of God?

> "When I enter into my pain rather than run from it, I will find at the center of my pain an amazing insight."
>
> John Powell

I was familiar with such hymns as "Victory in Jesus" and "Mansions over the Hilltop." I've sat under shiny metal crosses, beautifully carved wooden ones, and even some with purple satin draped ever so elegantly across them. In church we spoke in hushed tones and never ran. We wore our best suits or dresses—women never wore pants—and learned about Jesus, who wore white and loved the little children. Very young, we learned that Jesus now lives in heaven, seated at the right hand of the Father, where it is as shiny and beautiful as our crosses.

You can imagine my shock as a young impressionable teen at discovering churches who still cling to rough-hewn crucifixes, with Jesus still hanging, bleeding on them. A wise professor explained that people who live in conditions of suffering need a Savior who understands their pain. "Yes," he said, "they too serve a risen Savior, but they cry out to one who meets them in their daily agonies."

We've already addressed the question of why doesn't God do something if he knows everything. But here we wonder, if God knows of our suffering, does he care enough to get angry about it? Does he want to even the score? What do we read in the eyes of God? Are we expected to just hang our heads and bleed?

Dr. Gregory Boyer and I discussed wrestling with God. "It's engaging in hand-to-hand combat with Jesus, Doug," he said passionately. He found in his experience that only when we fully launch into the questions and haunting doubts can we ever find Jesus revealing his truth.

Dan Allender and Tremper Longman III compel us a step further.

> In the darkness of our emotional wrestling with God, we grow in our understanding of Him. When He does not respond to us as we expect, we learn about His surprising character . . . Further, our darkest emotions reveal something—though in a skewed, bent, and tarnished way—about God's emotional life. How can we begin to understand the nature of God's anger unless we enter into our own? How are we to gain any picture of what it means for a holy, righteous God to be jealous for His people if we ignore our human envy and jealousy?[2]

Is This God's Idea?

Some would say that God's plan allows evil to prey and feed on innocent people. Is God's design faulty? Does God understand the pain we carry as a result of his plan?

The Psalms propel us into these deepest questions about ourselves, about others, and about God. As we let them expose the depths of our emotion, they will lead us to the God who reveals his emotions in the midst of our struggle.

The vivid language of Psalms 12 and 13 verbalizes prayers for help when all mankind seems evil and every tongue lies. I hear the distress in King David's voice.

> Help, LORD, for the godly are no more;
>   the faithful have vanished from among men.
> Everyone lies to his neighbor;
>   their flattering lips speak with deception.
>
> Psalm 12:1–2

> Look on me and answer, O LORD my God.
>   Give light to my eyes, or I will sleep in death;
> my enemy will say, "I have overcome him,"
>   and my foes will rejoice when I fall.
>
> Psalm 13:3–4

If God feels this, surely he will do something. Right?

We ask again the question of whether God gets involved or simply stands by to let his children duke it out. Humanity has often taken vengeance into its own hands at the disillusionment that God didn't act quickly enough. We see what it has brought us.

Take Judas Iscariot, for example. Judas betrayed Jesus to the Roman authorities and religious leaders. Many wonder how Judas could have lived in the inner circle of Jesus' friends and disciples and still commit such a heinous act. A little detail in the Book of Mark might give us a clue. Judas went to the chief priests to betray Jesus *before* being offered a bribe. This suggests that Judas had some other motive besides money.

> "The tragedy of war is that it uses man's best to do man's worst."
>
> Harry Emerson Fosdick

Judas's treachery leads many to believe that he might have been an anti-Roman zealot who was disappointed that Jesus had not proved to be the rebel leader Judas expected. In other words, Judas was angry that Jesus didn't rise up to overthrow the Roman government as the mighty warrior the Jews anticipated in their coming Messiah.

How many Judases mark the pages of history? We strain hard against the urge to force the hand of God into action. When God doesn't respond as we wish, we often betray our faith or change our view of who or what God is.

Choose to Believe

Our inner turmoil escalates as we ponder this type of God. If God is personal and does feel, then we are at a crossroads of choice. Many of us would like to avoid confrontation or even acknowledge the possibility of a heartless God who doesn't act on our behalf as we wish he would. The easiest route might be to believe in a life force or a great spirit.

Pain and suffering produce a fork in the road.
It is not possible to remain unchanged.

To let others or circumstances dictate your future is to have
  chosen.
To allow pain to corrode your spirit is to have chosen.
And to be transformed into the image of Christ by these difficult and trying circumstances is to have chosen.

Tim Hansel

God created us with a will of our own. The beauty of this
design is that we can freely choose him and the path he has
designed for us. In his design for humanity, God empowered
us with an incredible range of movement within his creation.
Could it be that this power is both our ally and our foe? By
choice, humanity has accomplished profound advances as it
has bound itself together and survived many terrible dangers.
Civilizations have risen and fallen because people also make
choices that bring about evil and destructive results. Perhaps
our choices also warp our existential lens.

Dance, Dance, Dance

In his great design of life, God gave us a free will, which
includes relationships that live and breathe. A relationship exists
because two beings *want* it to exist. And like human relationships, we have the choice of slamming the door in God's face or
pressing in close to see what he will do next or where he will
lead us.

My wife, Stephanie, and I wanted to find a fun activity we could
share for the rest of our lives. We decided to do something fun
and foreign. I heard of a studio that taught salsa dancing and
talked my wife and another couple into going with us. Being white
and coming from conservative evangelical backgrounds, neither
of us had many skills or cultural rhythm to build on. (Some of
you are grinning . . . you know what I had to learn!) The salsa
dance is Latin. After eight weeks of twisting, turning, stumbling,
elbows in the eye, bruised wrists . . . we now love the dance!

In salsa, you cannot sloppily stand on the floor and just wiggle. You need to know how to move your feet, your hips, your

torso, and your "choulders." In some dance styles, you can have a partner who is not skilled and still enjoy the dance. Not here! Ladies, the man is the lead, and if he is horrible, you will either dance horribly too or be forced to take the lead yourself.

As I've learned to lead in this dance, I've discovered *leading* doesn't mean that I make all the choices. We both have to choose. Our choices are nonstop; for me what moves are coming next, and for my partner when to follow and when to initiate her own complementary moves. This dance is exhilarating! Why? Of course, the music is "the best." The intricate dialogue of split-second stimulus and response of partners, continually letting their wills say "yes" to one another, is amazing. He must lead with confident decision: "Yes, this is where I'm taking you." She must respond with equal confidence: "Yes, I will go there!" The result is great fun.

Life is a dance. When God granted us a will or choice, he asked us to dance with him and with one another. However, we have the choice to dance together or alone. In the studio of life, some will stand in the middle of the floor and wiggle and some will work diligently to perfect their individual performance. But solo dancers miss the thrill of harmony and cooperation between two partners and the creative energy that only comes after hours of sweat, disappointment, and frustration.

> "God asks no one whether he will accept life. This is not the choice. The only choice you have as you go through life is how you will live it."
>
> Bernard Meltzer

We do have another choice; we can refuse to dance altogether. We can stiffen to the harmonies and rhythm and just watch or stalk out the door. But the dance goes on, and we are given the invitation to join at any time.

Did God know what he was doing with this plan? Giving us the opportunity to choose empowers us to experience heaven or hell. Our choices will determine which path we take. I think God's nature required us to have that choice. Communion—an intimate attribute of God himself—requires active volition. With our choice comes human pain or pleasure. We chose it, or someone made a choice and we felt the effect of that choice.

In every moment opportunity exists for evil or good. Along with the beauty of choice in our relationships comes the pain in our relationships as well. *Beauty and terror are bed partners in the choices of humanity.*

Tears of God

God revealed himself through his Son, Jesus. Look at how God chose to express his emotion in a real-life situation.

Jesus' close friends included a family with two sisters and a brother. Their names were Martha, Mary, and Lazarus. Jesus spent lots of time with them—Martha probably made sure there was always something tasty to eat, and Mary was a great one to chat with. I'm certain Lazarus was congenial too, because he hosted Jesus and his disciples on several occasions.

When Jesus was traveling by the Jordan River, word came to him that his good friend Lazarus was sick. Strangely, Jesus decided to stay down near the river area rather than hurry to help his buddy. A true friend doesn't just "blow off" going to be with a friend who is deathly sick. A little baffled at first, the disciples must have thought, "Ah, can't fool us this time. We know you must be planning to heal Lazarus from off-site!"

After a few days, Jesus nonchalantly decided to head back to Bethany, where Lazarus's home was. You can imagine the shock of Jesus' followers when they arrived in Bethany only to hear mourners wailing. Lazarus had been dead for four days! They had even missed the funeral.

Both Martha and Mary believed that Jesus could have healed their brother. Can you imagine their disillusionment and anger? They'd seen him heal the sick before! They were deeply hurt that Jesus was too late.

Confused and embarrassed, the disciples had only their wrinkled brows and sackcloth to shroud the questions raging inside them. They didn't dare ask their accusing questions in front of Martha and Mary. They would have to wait until they were alone with Jesus. *Why did you wait? Why didn't you heal our friend . . . your friend? You waited for him to die! Why?* Maybe the bold and vocal Peter would ask, "Hey, Jesus, you did that on purpose! What's the deal?"

Jesus needed to proclaim to them and generations to follow that he is "the resurrection and the life." In the climactic miracle that was about to take place, Jesus demonstrated that he alone is the access to eternal life; so that even when you die, with Christ you live. Turning to the tomb, Jesus had the stone removed. With the authority of God himself, Jesus commanded Lazarus to come out of the tomb. Shrouded in grave clothes, Jesus' friend appeared!

A story with a great ending for sure, but how does it relate to God feeling our pain? Now that we know how the story ends, let's flip back a few pages. When Jesus saw Mary before he called Lazarus to life, the Scripture says,

> When Jesus saw her weeping, and the Jews who had come along with her also weeping, he was deeply moved in spirit and troubled. "Where have you laid him?" he asked. "Come and see, Lord," they replied. Jesus wept.

> John 11:33–35

Think about it. Why would God cry?

Jesus knew *in advance* what would take place. He knew Lazarus would die. He also knew this miracle would impact his ministry and declare him as the only access to God. He knew Lazarus would live again. So why cry?

When Jesus' eyes met with Mary's, he saw the incredible pain and agony of his dear friend and *it moved him deeply*. God came to earth clothed in a human body, not only so can we can follow his example in right living but so we can see how he tenderly responded to those around him.

God gave humankind a choice; to follow him or not. As a result of generations scarred by hate and selfish motive, we all will taste pain and suffering. The Creator not only gave us a symbol of his care, he showed his face by coming to us in the form of Jesus. And we can see him cry.

Does God feel the ache you carry? Oh yes, and much more. He helps lift it from you. "Cast all your care upon me," his words encourage. God alone knows the intimate details of your circumstance, and he feels your pain more wholly than any other. God cared so much that he sent the Holy Spirit, our promise of comfort, wisdom, and guidance. But how can God as spirit relate to our material world?

Look more closely and you'll find we too are spiritual beings. We are body, soul, and spirit. God became flesh so that he could be seen with physical eyes. Then God sent his Spirit to reside in each of us so we could see him with spiritual eyes. We don't search in vain to prove that God is real. "To search for the Spirit is like hunting for your eyeglasses while wearing them," says Philip Yancey. "The Spirit is what we perceive *with* rather than what we perceive, the One who opens our eyes to underlying *spirit*-ual realities."[3]

God hears our lament regarding the results in our lives from the poor choices of others. The good news is that we don't even have to know what to ask for. The Greek word for Holy Spirit, *paracletos*, means "one who stands beside." The Holy Spirit intercedes for us when we don't know how to respond to those who have hurt us. When we can only weep "with sighs too deep for words," the Holy Spirit tends to us at our side.

King David not only asks for God to help him; he also sings of God's unfailing love and protection from these people. "O Lord, you will keep us safe and protect us from such people forever" (Ps. 12:7). "But I trust in your unfailing love; my heart rejoices in your salvation. I will sing to the Lord, for he has been good to me" (Ps. 13:5–6). David found that in his despair and deep questions, God cares. The Creator feels our ache deeply and his love defies failure.

God is good because he has not only expressed his deep care for us in the face of Jesus, but also through his Spirit, who remains with us so that we may receive comfort directly from him.

The Last Call

Dancing partners do not look at one another's feet or hands; they lock into one another's gaze. The leader's face helps give the needed cues as he looks deeply into the face of his partner. As his body moves, the partner moves.

God is near. He will take the lead. Will you follow? Engage with him again in the spiritual dance of life. Of course, others will continue to make choices that hurt, but *we* also get a choice. We can choose to respond to this God who came in flesh and now remains with us.

Fix your eyes on his . . . and dance.

7

When God Is Silent, Are You to Blame?

In this chatty society, silence has become a very fearful thing. For most people, silence creates itchiness and nervousness. Many experience silence not as full and rich, but as empty and hollow.

For them silence is like a gaping abyss which can swallow them up.

Henri J. M. Nouwen

"Now I lay me down to sleep, I pray the Lord my soul to keep. If I should die before I wake, I pray the Lord my soul to take. God bless Mommy and Daddy, Grandma and Grandpa, Pastor and Mrs. Smith, and everybody! Amen."

Little children bedecked in flannel jammies pray words like these all across our nation. Don't you wish that you could still end your day with a simple rhyming prayer as you drift off to sleep without a care about tomorrow? Age crowds out these simple supplications. How old were you when you first asked, "Does God really hear me?" You must believe he does or you wouldn't pray at all. But when does God respond? What if he doesn't?

Because I learned to say the name "Jesus" before I could say "More, please," I was surprised to learn that a Unitarian friend has her little boy blow bubbles when he is frightened or concerned about nightmares. It seems so . . . empty. I must admit, though, there are times when my prayers feel as empty as bubbles. At least you can see where bubbles go before they pop.

When prayers seem to bounce off church rafters, we are left feeling cold and isolated. Home feels a bit safer so we turn to God again by our bedside. To our knees we go. After the "amen" we pause, hearing nothing. No applause or warm feelings enveloping us. *Did I say it wrong? How do I get God to respond?* Do you ever wonder?

Is This Silence from God Real?

"I'm so tired of this game, Doug! Why won't God talk to me? It feels like he's not there." I hear these words almost weekly. Whether I host a chat room or speak at conventions or church gatherings, people express their frustration to me about God's strange silence. Is it real? Oh yes.

In relationships, we are supposed to communicate. So when we sense silence from God, we experience a type of pain. The lack of communication confuses us. *If God loves me, why won't he talk to me?* We hate silence when it brings distance between us.

When I was young and newly married, I hated silence. My bride knew it well and used that to her advantage when we had an argument. We'd just be getting to the part of the argument where I had some "ammo" when she would turn and walk away, midsentence! I was outraged! To combat this silent treatment, I would follow her. In and out of rooms we'd parade until she went into the bathroom and closed the door behind her. I'd stand on the other side of the door, tapping my fingernails in irritating rhythm and continuing my discourse. I knew she couldn't take it long. *Whoosh!* The door would fly open and she'd passionately unload on me again. Although her sermons scathed me, I preferred to suffer her anger rather than bear her silence. Silence hurts.

One Christian woman wrote me, "I feel like I've been dead inside for a long time, Doug. Is there any hope for me? So many times I cry out to God for help. I used to be so close to him. He was my life."

What has changed in this woman's life? Not God, because he never changes. Yet there are times, it seems, when God doesn't reply to our prayers. Our cries for mercy and our pleas for him to draw close to our souls seem to go unheeded. And the silence shakes our very lives.

Introducing an Ancient Contemporary

I'd like to introduce you to a dear friend of mine. Although his name is unique, his story is quite common. His name is Job.

The Bible dedicates an entire book to this man and his story. Job is known as a "righteous man," meaning, in part, he was without blame. He did nothing wrong in his life to deserve pain or suffering, yet both were his lot in life.

Job was a very wealthy man with a loving wife and many children. He and his entire estate were esteemed in his homeland, and he was sought after for counsel among many. Then one day God permitted a tragedy to strip Job of all he had. Follow this gripping story with me.

> One day when Job's sons and daughters were feasting and drinking wine at the oldest brother's house, a messenger came to Job and said, "The oxen were plowing and the donkeys were grazing nearby, and the Sabeans attacked and carried them off. They put the servants to the sword, and I am the only one who has escaped to tell you!"
>
> While he was still speaking, another messenger came and said, "The fire of God fell from the sky and burned up the sheep and the servants, and I am the only one who has escaped to tell you!"
>
> While he was still speaking, another messenger came and said, "The Chaldeans formed three raiding parties and swept down on your camels and carried them off. They put the servants to the sword, and I am the only one who has escaped to tell you!"

While he was still speaking, yet another messenger came and said, "Your sons and daughters were feasting and drinking wine at the oldest brother's house, when suddenly a mighty wind swept in from the desert and struck the four corners of the house. It collapsed on them and they are dead, and I am the only one who has escaped to tell you!"

Job 1:13–19

As Job reeled under the weight of the news, I'm sure he wondered how life could possibly get any worse. But it did get worse. Soon afterward Job was afflicted with painful sores from the top of his head to the soles of his feet. Without pride or self-honor, Job took a place among the ashes to sit in misery. His wife even came to him and said, "Are you still holding on to your integrity? Curse God and die!" (Job 2:9). When your own wife wants you to turn on God, that's bad. When she wants you to just give up and die so she can bury you, you've reached the bottom of the barrel. And Job had reached it.

Soon friends came to him. They sat with him and offered counsel. For endless days they sought to answer the question, "Why?" Job shared his thoughts as well. It seemed God was not answering Job's prayers. He too was experiencing silence from God.

Yet he began to press an audience with God. He replied to his friends, "My eyes have seen all this, my ears have heard and understood it. What you know, I also know; I am not inferior to you. *But I desire to speak to the Almighty and to argue my case with God*" (Job 13:1–3, author's emphasis). Turning to God, he prayed, "I cry out to you, O God, but you do not answer; I stand up, but you merely look at me" (Job 30:20).

An ancient man was Job, yes. But his struggle was very contemporary.

Nights Dark and Quiet

Silence falls like a crushing blow to our spirit. Our inner design is to communicate with one another. Just as we long for an open loving relationship with our parents, we were created to communicate with our Maker. When we experience this drought of interaction, our inner being writhes in anguish and loneliness.

When the silence comes from someone we love, confusion and frustration amplify the pain. Even as I screamed to what felt like empty rafters, I knew that God was there. He would never leave. All we want is his voice. To have him simply clear his throat would be a welcome surprise.

Maybe your heart feels like an orphaned child or a dark, echoing church. Perhaps you understand this silence as you receive it from others. Listen to my dear friend's heart in such a circumstance.

Have you ever poured your heart out in a letter or an e-mail without ever receiving a response back? I have. After years of misunderstandings and separation from my dad, I wrote him a letter expressing all my past anger and pain, and my renewed hope for resolution. I hoped for something . . . anything. My old ideals of building a new friendship were put away. I traded them in for a more realistic package. All I wanted now was to forgive and simply move forward as two adults with some understanding of one another. I only wanted him to acknowledge me.

Do you know what I received in return? Silence.

Silence! I gave him the benefit of the doubt. I gave time another chance. I filled my calendar with events and my life with people to keep my mind off of the nagging ache that now formed a knot—an emotional tumor, you might say. I wondered how many days of silence should go by before I tagged the relationship as a lost cause. *No!* This was my dad. Our relationship could not be a lost cause. I must have said or done something wrong. Perhaps the letter only made things worse.

To add to my mounting frustration, my other siblings carry on a fine relationship with our father. In fact, my brother spends a couple of hours a week on the phone with him! And when I try to bring up the subject with my mother, she disregards my concern, seemingly oblivious to any strain. Am I to blame?

Silence in any relationship can choke away our breath. Like a naive child waiting, his nose pressed against the frosted windowpane of an orphanage, we often view silence from God as betrayal or rejection. We wait for any "glimpse" of our Father, and when no figure darkens the door of our existence, we feel alone.

Maybe this is why David wrote, "To you I call, O LORD my Rock; do not turn a deaf ear to me. For if you remain silent, I will be like those who have gone down to the pit [grave]" (Ps. 28:1). In David's eventful life, the one thing that caused him the deepest pain was for his God to remain silent. Without the voice of God, David felt like a dead man walking.

When God is silent, we often begin questioning ourselves, our motives, our discipline, our sin . . . the list goes on. We can't see God and therefore can't read his actions or his intent. It is natural to ask, "When God is silent, am I to blame?"

I believe God's character and ways are so beyond our comprehension that our asking if we are to blame is like a child wondering if she were to blame for a lightning storm. Philip Yancey assures his reader in *Reaching for the Invisible God*, "If God merely wanted to make his existence known to every person on earth, God would not hide. However, the direct presence of God would inevitably overwhelm our freedom. . . . God wants a different kind of knowledge, a personal knowledge that requires a commitment from the one who seeks to know him."[1] Yancey goes on to share words of John Updike, "The sensation of silence cannot be helped: a loud and evident God would be a bully, an insecure tyrant, an all-crushing datum instead of, as he is, a bottomless encouragement to our faltering and frightened being."[2] As I reflect and ponder God's moments of silence, I closely connect with his parent role in training us in the path we should go.

Four Reasons God Is Silent

When my children ask me questions, I don't always answer them immediately. I often wait. I remain silent, but I do so for a purpose. Similarly, I believe God remains silent at times with specific intent.

Silence from God Punctuates His Message

A favorite author of mine, Henri Nouwen, describes one of his trips through Los Angeles when he had a sensation of driving through a huge dictionary. "Wherever I looked there were words trying to take my eyes from the road. They said, 'Use me, take me, buy me, drink me, smell me, touch me, kiss me, and sleep with me.' In such a world, who can maintain a respect for words?"[3]

What a stark contrast to Nouwen's life. He meticulously tailored each of his words to carry heavy freight. Every word was so carefully chosen that a single paragraph, a sentence, or a simple phrase can stand alone in profound truth. How interesting it is to discover that in spite of his love of words, Nouwen often felt inundated with them, until "words had all but lost their meaning."

> "Silence is but a rich pause in the music of life."
>
> Sarojini Naidu

> "Wherever we go we are surrounded by words," exclaimed Henri Nouwen. "Words softly whispered, loudly proclaimed, or angrily screamed; words spoken, recited, or sung; words on records, in books, on walls, or in the sky; words in many sounds, many colors, or many forms; words to be heard, read, seen, or glanced at; words which flicker off and on, move slowly, dance, jump, or wiggle. Words, words, words! They form the floor, the walls, and the ceiling of our existence."[4]

It's time for a timeout! I never really appreciated timeouts until I became a parent. Sadly many parents and educators misunderstand timeouts to be punishment. Spiritually speaking, they are fine for discipline, but God does not use them for punishment. He never sticks us off in the corner by ourselves for our wrongdoing or until he regains control of his anger. God uses timeouts in the same way parents do—for a reason.

I'll never forget one day when my son was three. I had something loving and kind to share with him, but he was determined to have his way. He became so frustrated that he collapsed on the floor, throwing such an outrageous fit that he would have never heard me. Gently but firmly I sat him down on the step. I held him there until he sat quietly. Then I remained silent until he was calm enough to hear my voice. I realized in that moment with my son that I too had felt constricted by God's hand in the midst of silence. Now I understand why.

There are times when we need to echo God's silence. We must wait quietly so God can finally speak to us. His message to us has a stronger voice when we remain quiet with him first. "The Word of God is born out of the eternal silence of God," said Nouwen. God will not force himself upon us, nor burn his words into our spirit. God's words carry much weight. We must give our full attention so he can share his great love for us. It is his silence that often punctuates his important and timely message.

God's Silence Drives Our Spiritual Roots Deep

What would happen if people took time routinely to reflect deeply about their lives? What benefits could revolutionize our society? How marvelous to have people focus solely on their relationship with the great God who created them.

Silence from God often affords this. It forces us to think deeply about the priorities in life and the role we play in this cosmic existence. There is another reason I believe God is silent. It is what I call "the power of drought."

Some time ago, I found an abundance of mushrooms growing in my yard. I sprayed weed killer and fertilized the rich green grass, but these mushrooms seemed relentless! Finally I called a lawn specialist. In less than three minutes, he summed up my problem. "You are watering too much," he said. "The grass needs seasons of drought for the roots to grow deep. The drought will get rid of the fungus and prevent the roots from rotting."

When I sought God with my whole heart and longed for him to speak to me, I experienced a spiritual drought of sorts, which drove my spiritual roots deep into the soil of my beliefs. I began to examine everything I did and said as a Christian. I began to ask why I believe what I do. In my hungry search for God's existence, I examined all my long-held, innermost beliefs for reality and truth. Like King David, I sought God . . . relentlessly.

The result of that silence, or drought, was the strengthening of my spiritual roots. They dug deep into the Scriptures. They found life at such depths. Today I can truly stand on a faith that is stronger than ever before because of that season of silence from God. While it was not pleasant, it was indeed healthy.

God's Silence Shapes Us

> "Lord, teach me to silence my own heart that I may listen to the gentle movement of the Holy Spirit within me and sense the depths which are of God."
>
> Elijah de Vidas

Have you ever watched a potter shape clay on the wheel? It is a most amazing process, and for our thoughts on silence, it offers rich insight. Before the potter ever adds water to the clay, he has a purpose in mind as to what he desires to create. First the right amount of silt is mixed with water. Then the clay is kneaded again and again to remove all air bubbles. Finally it is placed in the very center of the wheel and it begins to spin.

When the potter presses his hands with gentle strength against the clay, shaping immediately begins to occur. Soon the potter finishes the piece and trims it neatly. However, there is still one vital step. This vessel cannot be used until it has been fired. Under intense heat, the shaped clay grows strong and solid. Silt and water fuse, making an impermeable and lasting substance.

If you were that vessel, what would you be thinking? These would be my thoughts: I was all right with the squeezing and flexing. After all, I could feel the potter's hands wrapped around me. But it's dark in here. It's silent, and whew! . . . it's hot . . . and the potter is nowhere to be found.

I'm quite certain I'd soon be shouting to that potter, "Get me out of here! It's hot and I've had it! I've already got my shape! Let me o-u-t!" But the potter waits. The process requires time and heat. To remove the vessel any earlier would abort its completion.

But here is the hope: The potter will not let the clay remain in the kiln any longer than necessary. How do we know? Because it was created for a purpose.

Many times God will be silent to shape us. Whether he allows the heat to boil the toxins from our system or to perfect us for a greater purpose, he has a plan.

God's Silence May Be Our Inability to See the Big Picture

There is a story told of a clipper ship that had to navigate its way through some treacherous waters in a narrow channel. To complicate matters, heavy low fog had rolled in and prevented the captain from seeing where to turn.

Up in the crow's nest atop the main mast, a lone sailor could see both banks of the channel. He began yelling directions down to the captain. "Starboard, five degrees! Now steady! Hold!" Then silence.

We can only imagine the anxiety within the captain and crew after the "hold" command. They could not see where they were going. But silence from the crow's nest meant one thing: They were on course. If any change of direction was needed, they would hear the order. Until then they were to hold the course.

Our spiritual walk is often like that clipper ship. When God directs us, we hear his voice beautifully. Then comes a period of silence. We wonder why he won't respond. In truth, it may be because we are doing fine. If God would answer audibly, he might just say, "You are on course. Hold fast!"

You may find yourself in a foggy channel trying to navigate life. Perhaps you too sense your life being pressed painfully and firmly onto a rough table by the hand of God. In those times when you call to him and he responds in silence, know that he loves you still. Stay the course! Trust God's plan! He will guide you through and make you stronger in the meantime.

God Speaks

Just when your maturity allows you to wait calmly during God's silence, you will find him speaking to you in ways you've never dreamed. God's voice is fresh and often full of delightful surprises. How marvelous it is to get a surprise from God, especially after a period of silence!

A dear friend of mine had experienced severe exhaustion in his career. In fact, he had worked tirelessly as a pastor of a church only to find more hurting people. He shared with me the hopeless sense of the work at times. In the midst of it all, he felt that perhaps God had forgotten him.

Ready to cash it all in, he left the office late one afternoon. As he stepped out the doors, he was comforted with the most beautiful view he had ever seen. Before him on the horizon was the largest and most vivid rainbow, the very symbol of God's promise that he will never forget us.

"I just stood there and cried," he told me. At that moment, God spoke to his heart through the beauty of his creation. It was a welcome surprise indeed.

> "There is hardly ever a complete silence in our soul. God is whispering to us well-nigh incessantly. Whenever the sounds of the world die out in the soul, or sink low, then we hear these whisperings of God. He is always whispering to us, only we do not always hear because of the noise, hurry, and the distraction that life causes as it rushes on."
>
> Frederick William Faber

When we stop to smell a rose or inhale the fragrance after a fresh rain, we may be surprised to hear God break his silence. While the creation is not the Creator, his fingerprints and voice abound there.

The Voice of Presence

A young lady e-mailed me a brief note following a youth retreat. "The night before we all went up I was so frustrated with God and angry that I couldn't hear him talking to me, but I heard him speak last weekend through you. The retreat was just what I needed to keep me going."

There are times when God speaks to us without words. Rather, he uses the lives of others to be his voice. In a similar way to how God spoke through my ministry to this teen girl, God may speak to you.

Children often are a delightful tool that God uses to speak to us. We love how their naive minds and uninhibited actions often cause them to speak or do what we could only wish to get away with. I have learned as a minister and as a father that often in those humorous or touching moments, I hear something unique. We may hear the voice of God as a lesson, or possibly verbatim, but God sometimes speaks best when he speaks through a child.

There have been times in my life when I desperately needed God to speak to me through the lives of others. In times of deep suffering I had no interest in their wisdom or opinions. In fact, I didn't even want to hear them speak. I just wanted their *presence*.

> "He who does not understand your silence will probably not understand your words."
>
> Elbert Green Hubbard

The ministry of presence is incredibly vital. Remember our friend Job? In his great distress, three friends came and wept with him. For an entire week, they sat by him and said nothing. They were doing well until they began speaking. Their words brought no comfort or explanation to Job. In fact, their words angered him! He even responded to them, "You are worthless physicians, all of you! If only you would be altogether silent! For you, that would be wisdom" (Job 13:4–5).

How I have wanted to quote that verse to those who fire off cheap opinions! We do not need words. Most of the time, we just need a friend to be there for us. God uses their presence to speak to us. As I look back on the time in the hospital during the deaths of my wife and daughter, what I value most is not the conversations or advice, and not even the prayers. Instead, I remember the people. The fact that they were there touches me deeply even today.

A Gentle Nudge

If you have been married for any length of time, you will understand this form of communication. It is called the gentle nudge. Now, I'm not speaking of the nudge you get under the table when you embarrass yourself in front of company. Those nudges aren't so gentle anyway! This nudge carries greater depth and meaning.

Some years ago I sat in a church service listening to a pastor. He was speaking about how we often feel as if God may be finished with us, that our purpose seems to be empty. Eloquently this minister touched my soul and brought me to understand that God is never finished with us. In fact, he has a great plan for each of us. Turning to my wife with tears in my eyes, I simply squeezed her hand. No words were exchanged, but in that brief moment we conversed intimately.

When Dan Rather interviewed Mother Teresa some time ago, he asked her what she said to God when she prayed. "I don't say anything. I listen," she replied. He then asked her what she heard God say. "He doesn't say anything," she said. "He listens."[5]

If God seems silent to you, I encourage you to draw nearer to his heart. Get close enough to sense his presence and feel his pulse. You may not need his words. You may just need to feel his breath on your face, or a simple nudge that says, *I'm still here with you!* What a great surprise to feel God when you have asked to hear him.

> "The fruit of prayer is a deepening of faith. And the fruit of faith is love. And the fruit of love is service. But to be able to pray, we need silence. Silence of the heart. The soul needs time to go away and pray; to use the mouth, to use the eyes, to use the whole body. And if we don't have that silence, then we don't know how to pray."
>
> Mother Teresa

Deep within There Stirs the Spirit

Our inner core is not hollow. Within your being is that part of you that is spirit. Hopefully your spirit abides with the Spirit of God, bringing you contentment and the joy of life. This center is deeper than the soul that comprises your logic, emotions, and will.

It is in this place that we sense the "still small voice" of God whispering to us. "Is that me or is that God?" I've been asked.

It could be either, or both. From the Spirit of God comes the fresh wind of his voice. It blows into our spirit and through our conscience. From there it filters through our logic, will, and emotions, as we process our thoughts.

Many times these gentle whispers of God are so vague we wonder if it is truly him. Using Scripture, we can judge its validity and holy source. When finding that these soft winds are from God, we can rejoice in the communion with our Creator. He does speak to us.

Black and White in Color

Many of us have read Bible verses so many times that we tend to skim through familiar areas. Stop! God may surprise you in those common passages. Take time to *experience* the context of the passage. Try to activate your five senses within the text. Study the culture and time period of the story.[6]

I have heard preachers who are *gifted* at making the Bible boring. How tragic! The Scriptures are filled with such wonderful stories and truth. To extract the life from the Book and then transmit the remaining sediment to an audience is to me a sin. The same holds true for us who read it. Don't fly through the passages just to mark off your daily reading. It is better to break the Bread of Life and taste it than to gulp it down whole.

God will surprise you regularly as you read his inspired words. Spend time in the Scriptures. Read until you come to a place where you ask "Why?" and then stay there until God reveals the answer. It may only be a few words at a time. Memorize a paragraph and meditate on it for a week or month. I memorized James 1:2–4 and meditated on that passage alone for nearly three months. The depth of understanding about joy and suffering that I received there is invaluable and will remain with me forever.

Open the Book once again. Start in the Gospels and experience Jesus afresh. Perhaps you would like to learn more of the ancient poet and king of Israel, David, as we've shared in each chapter. You will find the setup to his story beginning in 1 Samuel. Wherever you begin, just dig in, carry on, and taste.

Once Again with Job

Poor old Job. He had lost everything and his friends gave horrid advice. Finally God broke the silence and addressed Job personally. But it was far from refreshing or beautiful. In fact, God speaks verse upon verse about how complex and beyond understanding he is. One would think it arrogant, I suppose, for God to applaud his greatness while Job is suffering and only wants answers. But God is . . . well, God! After this great discourse, Job responds to the Creator with words of insight for us.

> Surely I spoke of things I did not understand, things too wonderful for me to know. . . . My ears had heard of you but now my eyes have seen you. Therefore I despise myself and repent in dust and ashes.
>
> Job 42:3b, 5–6

How I wish Job and I could have dinner together! What a great experience it would be to learn from the man who demanded an audience with God and got it. He humbled himself before the Almighty, realizing that God's silence was based on an understanding too great for Job to comprehend. When he finally saw God, he didn't have a list of questions to ask as many of us think we will in heaven. No, he repented and humbled himself.

God Will Speak to You

Dear friend, God will speak to you. Silence comes for many reasons. And when that silence is broken, the display of God's heart to you will be marvelous.

Be prepared to hear him. Do not let anger or bitterness cloud your "ears." Keep your life open to any new expression of your Father. Open the Scriptures again and begin listening in new ways.

To help you begin, read portions of Psalm 27. Join with the heart of King David and worship our God who is good and loves you enough to remain silent for the right time and the right reason. Speak your heart to God, fight, and then rest in God's silence.

> To you I call, O Lord my Rock;
>   do not turn a deaf ear to me.
> For if you remain silent,
>   I will be like those who have gone down to the pit.
> Hear my cry for mercy
>   as I call to you for help.[7]
>
>   Psalm 28:1–2a

With renewed assurance of God's eternal love and goodness, David ends this psalm:

> I am still confident of this:
>   I will see the goodness of the Lord
>   in the land of the living.
> Wait for the Lord;
>   be strong and take heart
>   and wait for the Lord.
>
>   Psalm 27:13–14

8

Why Is God Not Fair?

Without the bitter, I'd not know how good is the sweet.

Tracey McBride

He ran upstairs from the basement crying in a panic.

"Mommy! Mo-o-om! Bri won't let me play my way!"

Luc, our youngest child, was trying to get along with the all-girl cast of friends in the basement. He was trying hard too, it seemed. When he rounded the corner, he was wearing lavender butterfly wings with fuzzy edging and glitter throughout. The small group of adults upstairs roared in laughter when they saw the little tearstained "angel." But he did not see the situation as humorous at all.

"Mom," he said, climbing into the safety of Stephanie's arms, "Brianna won't let me play the way I want to play. It's not fair!"

Children are born with an innate sense of fairness, and we never quit longing for it. As soon as a small child is aware of another little human playing next to him, he will begin to size the other little guy up. What child hasn't compared her dolls, clothes, or ice cream to those around her? When the slightest discrepancy is detected, her "unfair meter" goes ballistic.

As adults we struggle with the same issue. However, we've dressed it up in various packages and terms. Our "unfair meter" buzzes more quietly perhaps, but when your buddy gets a new truck and you're stuck with the old Tercel, doesn't it grate at you? And what about the couple who just bought that large new home. They don't even know what it's like to have to work because they were born with a "silver spoon in their mouth." "Keeping up with the Joneses" is a life lesson we learned at age two!

Green-Eyed Monsters

I admit, when I see someone living the lifestyle I long for, especially when they are arrogant, something powerful stirs deep inside. It's the rumbling of the old "green-eyed monster." The business world anticipates jealousy and even encourages it. If it motivates people to push harder—then it serves a good purpose, right?

Our human nature, which prompts us to cry, "Unfair!" influences how we view ourselves in relationship to others. How can we stay on the spiritual course when others strut through society with health, wealth, and upward mobility? Some folks are nice enough. But what about those who are driven beyond the point of integrity and honesty straight into the face of evil?

Americans didn't invent drug trafficking, prostitution, or the web of corporate crimes that slash our national and world economy. Listen to the description the psalmist gives of those his nation had to compete with in the ancient civilization during King David's reign.

> They wear pride like a jeweled necklace,
>   and their clothing is woven of cruelty.
> These fat cats have everything
>   their hearts could ever wish for!

They scoff and speak only evil;
   in their pride they seek to crush others.
They boast against the very heavens,
   and their words strut throughout the earth.
And so the people are dismayed and confused,
   drinking in all their words.
"Does God realize what is going on?" they ask.
   "Is the Most High even aware of what is happening?"
Look at these arrogant people—
   enjoying a life of ease while their riches multiply.

                                Psalm 73:6–12 NLT

We can feel justified in our anger. Well, almost. The flip side of "unfair" is just as troubling for those of us who are concerned about sharing a life in community. What are we to do when we see a cold, steely glance from others who keep us at a distance because of their own jealousy toward us?

The Beast of Bitterness

Have you ever met someone holding a grudge? It amazes me how people can spend so much energy on the offense. I hate being miserable, so I can't stay upset very long. But I have met people who have cursed and renounced family or other ties to their grave. I am baffled at how people do it! If only they would move beyond their bitterness toward health. Bitterness is not only distasteful, but in relationships it is severe and distressing to the mind, the body, and the soul and all those who come in contact with it. The energy people waste nursing such intense animosity could be redirected toward developing far greater relationships than the one at stake. They could really live, but they don't care. Having crashed their own pity party, they sign for a club membership to a life of resentment.

If you're one of these bound by bitterness, you may be fuming, "Yeah, what do you know about people who have done me wrong?" If you find that an offense has pushed you beyond pain or jealousy and you're creeping into the zone of bitterness, take heed.

Several years ago, I was a credentialed minister. At that time my late wife, Evon, was still living with AIDS, and our daughter had already died of the same disease. The source of their illness was an infected transfusion made by an HIV-positive male who was careless, if not deceitful, in his blood donation. I was attending my denomination's national conference in Portland, Oregon, and found myself sitting alone in a stadium of thousands. The crowds drank in every word of passionate preaching and celebrated with exuberant singing. At one point, a video with testimony after victorious testimony poured onto a huge screen.

> "No man can think clearly when his fists are clenched."
>
> George Jean Nathan

One of these testimonies included the story of an inner-city program. The leader shared of how marvelously God was providing for their ministry. He then shared of the miracles that had been occurring in their city as well. I froze motionless to my chair as this leader shared how a young man who was involved in prostitution and intravenous drug use had come into the center. "We prayed for him and he received Jesus. Not only did this man get saved, but he had been HIV-positive and God completely healed him!"

The crowd erupted in excited praise. I sat silent. I had prayed relentlessly for God to heal my innocent two-year-old daughter from AIDS. He didn't. My wife, who had dedicated her whole life to helping others, was now confined to her bed, struggling to breathe as her body fought respiratory infections due to the AIDS virus.

After I left the stadium I went to my room to call and check on my wife. A message had just arrived from a friend. "Call the hospital immediately! Evon took a bad turn. You need to fly home tonight."

I caught a red-eye flight home and hurried to the hospital. I walked into the waiting room and found my mother there. Her eyes were tender and compassionate. Mine were not. I was seething as I walked with her toward Evon's room. Glaring, I turned to my mom, "You want to know what I heard at General Council? God evidently healed a male prostitute and IV-drug user from AIDS." I looked at the room that contained my terminally ill wife. "He won't heal Ashli or Evon, but he will heal a male prostitute?!"

My soul screamed, "NOT FAIR!"

As we see it, life certainly is not fair. As long as we live, we will yell at the heavens that life is unfair. And as long as we believe in a God that is in control, we will raise one eyebrow to this Deity and question his fairness.

> Surely God is good
>> to . . . those who are pure in heart.
> But as for me, my feet had almost slipped;
>> I had nearly lost my foothold.
> For I envied the arrogant
>> when I saw the prosperity of the wicked.
> They have no struggles;
>> their bodies are healthy and strong.
> They are free from the burdens common to man;
>> they are not plagued by human ills.
>
>> Psalm 73:1–5

> Surely in vain have I kept my heart pure;
>> in vain have I washed my hands in innocence.
> All day long I have been plagued;
>> I have been punished every morning.
>
>> verses 13–14

> Then I realized how bitter I had become,
>> how pained I had been by all I had seen.
> I was so foolish and arrogant—
>> I must have seemed like a senseless animal to you.
>
>> verses 21–22 NLT

These words echo my confession even though they were written thousands of years ago. This portion of Psalm 73, though ancient in its composition, is always contemporary. Why? Humanity is unchanged.

It's Not the Same

Fair does not mean "same."

It is an elementary concept that we have to teach our kids as soon as we have more than one child. Ali has twin boys at age four. Her entire day consists of playing referee to determine that all is fair—the same—or convincing the boys that it doesn't need to be. But as the boys grow they each develop unique needs, and fair will no longer mean the same.

Parents of teenagers chuckle as they understand this all too well. How you treat one child may not be the same way you treat another. "That's not fair!" they scream. "Amber didn't have to come in that early!" The wise parent knows to mete out different amounts of reward and discipline based on the teens' individual needs.

No, fair does not mean "same" for our children. Neither does it for us as adults. It seems so obvious, but why does this question of fairness still haunt us at age thirty-five or fifty? We long for equality. However, getting the same as someone else does *not* equate with fairness. For example, if your neighbor cheats and treats his employees badly, and yet he enjoys a better lifestyle than you who've worked hard and honest, you certainly wouldn't consider his standard of living as fair.

Some years ago, a team of college guys sanded and restained the sides of my home and deck. These five young men had various personality styles and assorted work ethics. I told them I would pay them a flat fee as a group, divided by the number of men working.

The first day, everyone showed up and grabbed a sander. They worked feverishly most of the day. Come midafternoon, Dan was missing. When Rad, the leader of the crew, went looking for Dan, he found him chatting with Stephanie in the garage. Rad sharply barked orders for Dan to get back to work.

The next day, Dan and another guy did tasks that were more menial. Rad and Sean had to carry most of the work weight. As the third and fourth days progressed, it seemed that most of these men were suddenly obligated with other appointments, leaving Rad and Sean with more to do. They worked hard nonetheless and completed the house in a week.

On payday, all five showed up! Rad and Sean were quite upset that I still intended to pay everyone the same. "It's not fair!" they argued. "We did most of the work!" The others defended themselves, saying, "We worked, just not up on the ladders." As they argued, I had a tough decision to make. Should I fulfill my word and pay them all the same? Would that be fair?

Our desire for equality touches many areas of our lives: racial, gender, economic. Rather than asking why God is not fair in these areas, we must realize that it is man who is not fair. We were not born on an even playing field. What a rude awakening it is for children in the United States to discover that they really cannot be all they want to be. How many children really have a chance at being president? The goods have not been distributed equally. This primal demand for fairness stems from our inborn desire for justice.

And Justice for All

We long for what is just, whether it's the rules to a game, a paycheck for our labor, healing, or a home. Having been created in the image of God, we long for justice that can only be found in our Creator.

As a child, I had to stand every morning in our small country schoolhouse and recite the Pledge of Allegiance. Without even thinking, I can quote it today. Take a minute and recite it to yourself. Remember that last prepositional phrase? "With liberty and justice for all!" Now *that*, my friends, is a pledge. I will sign up any day for a country that can deliver its promise of being "indivisible, under God, with freedom . . . and not only that, but *justice* for all." And do we have it? Ask any lawyer.

Courthouses are packed with people in line for justice. They want what is theirs. They want their fair share and they want it now. Justice is not only sought, it is demanded. Demanded at least by the plaintiff. The guilty long for justice to look the other way.

"God's mill grinds slow, but sure."

George Herbert

We all want what is reasonably ours. We are not ones to ask for the moon, but we certainly want what is right. We want justice in the courts. We want justice to rule our local schools, our churches, and our homes.

Why?

"It's only fair."

Philip Yancey in his book *Disappointment with God* echoes this fact.

> The primal desire for fairness dies hard, and it should. Who among us does not sometimes yearn for more justice in this world here and now? Secretly, I admit, I yearn for a world "fault-proof" against disappointment. . . . But if I stake my faith on such a fault-proof earth, my faith will let me down. Even the greatest miracles do not resolve the problems of this earth. . . . We need more than a miracle. We need a new heaven and a new earth, and until we have those, unfairness will not disappear.[1]

Possessions, freedoms, pleasures—all must be reckoned with, and sometimes the cries of "not fair" come from places beyond the playground or living room. Often it's our soul that cries out. When we endure deep personal suffering, we look beyond the people around us and ask, "Why is God doing this to me? Why is God not fair?"

These were the words gasped over and over by a dear friend of Donna's. As a result of breaking his neck in a diving accident a couple of weeks prior to his high school graduation, Donna's friend Jonathan is a quadriplegic.

Approximately a decade later, Jon now speaks passionately about his gratitude for the life God has given him. Each day is still filled with intense frustrations and lots of pain. But even

though the frustrations never go away, Jon's bitterness has sub-
sided, and he has since come to the resolve that "God gives each
person a 'bag of tricks [tools]' for this journey through life."
Confident, Jon says, "though each of us has different 'goodies
in our bag' they all weigh the same . . . because God is just."

~

"Daddy, where are we going?" Joshua asked nervously. He
was about to be enrolled in kindergarten. First he needed his
inoculations. By this time we had lived in Colorado for two
years. Little Ashli was nineteen months old, and both she and
Evon were increasingly ill. Joshua loved to ride along with me
in my truck, but today he knew something was different.

At four years of age, Joshua was quite perceptive. On this particular day he noticed that we were not headed to the mall or
the church. Instead, we were driving by large office buildings
and complexes. To him, this was intriguing, confusing, and
nerve-wracking, because they looked *a lot* like the buildings
where the doctor's office was. Since Mommy and Ashli were not
in the truck, that meant one thing: *He* was the patient. And to
him, being the patient meant needles, pain, and lots of crying.

With a hint of fear, he again asked, "Daddy, where are we
going?"

I tried to be casual. "We're going to the doctor's office, Josh."

"B-but why? Why are we going to the doctor's office?"

I didn't want to tell him the whole truth. You parents may
understand my dilemma. How do you break the news to an
inquisitive child that pain is in his imminent future? I thought I
might fake him out with a complex-sounding answer. "You need
an inoculation, Josh."

"What's an inoculation?" The fear was not gone.

I was trying to be creative. Think, Doug! What is an inoculation? Don't scare him. Don't lie. Be creative. Think! You can do it.

"Uh . . . that's a shot, Josh." *Wow. What brilliance.*

I guessed his response correctly. Tears flowed freely as Josh
scooted his bottom into a protective posture against the pas-
senger door. "I don't want a shot, Daddy. I don't *want* a shot."

I tried ineptly to explain the necessity of inoculation. "Josh, they are going to give you an inactive form of a bacteria. It will go into your body and build up antibodies. . . ." Right over his head. He couldn't get past the needle. Josh continued to assert his right to protest. Our conversation lasted all the way into the doctor's office. "I'm not sick. I don't need a shot, Daddy. You love me, don't you? Please, Daddy. I don't want a shot!"

At the office the doctor prepared the needle and we turned Josh facedown on the padded examination table. "It's going to be all right," I reassured him. His whimpering crescendoed into a full cry.

I don't know who was more tense—Josh, me, the nurse, or the doctor. It took three of us to keep him on the table. The nurse pinned his arms down, and I held his head steady. Dr. Meyer leaned over his kicking legs and bared Joshua's backside. In one quick movement, he administered the shot.

When they stuck him with the needle, Josh looked straight at me. Looking deep into my eyes as I firmly held his head, he cried, "Daddy!" It was only one word, but his look said a million words. "Daddy, why the pain? Ouch, Daddy! Why are you letting them hurt me? I thought you were my father! It's not my fault. Why, Daddy? I thought you loved me."

Josh's face reflected pain. It showed fear. But he also had a startling look of disappointment—like I had let him down.

My eyes burned with tears as my mind suddenly raced to the familiar phrases I had uttered months before. "Why, God? I thought you loved me! I thought you were my Father! Why, Daddy? Why?"

Suddenly I heard a voice. Not an audible voice; but very clearly God spoke to my heart at that moment. He simply said, "It's the same with you and me."

A new understanding of who God is flooded my heart. You see, if I could explain the full reason for the inoculation to my son, I would. I love him. I would die for him. But even if I explained it, he wouldn't grasp it. For he can only understand simple, concrete thought. Until his mind matures, he can't understand abstract thoughts such as eternity . . . inertia . . . inoculation!

So it is with our heavenly Father. While we can handle some complex thoughts, God is divine. He is *all*-knowing! His level of thought so exceeds our own that we can never fully understand why he acts as he does. Yet if he could explain all the answers to our whys, he would. Right now, the answers would go right over our heads and we would label them "illogical." Many circumstances in life don't make sense. But that does not mean he does not love us. He does. So much so, that he would die for us . . . and did.

I picked up Josh and held him. "It's okay, Josh. Daddy loves you. I'm sorry that hurt. It's going to be okay. Daddy's here. Daddy loves you." With every word I said to Josh, I could see the tearstained face of my Father in heaven reassuring me of his love for me. I hugged Joshua and sensed God holding me and stroking my wounded soul, whispering strength and affection into my spirit.

It was then that my faith began rebuilding. I knew I was going to make it. While there was much I did not understand, I knew my Father in heaven loved me.[2]

You see, I found myself in the place of the Father. My son could not see how his receiving a shot was fair. How could his loving daddy order the pain? I ordered it because I knew more than he could comprehend. I knew the issues of inoculation and the decreased risks of infection once inoculated. I knew he couldn't attend kindergarten without the shot. It seemed fair to me but not to my son.

The Illogical Gap

If God is omniscient, meaning he knows all, then we must realize that we are not. We have great mental abilities, but we can never be equal to God in intelligence. Therefore, we will never fully understand the mind or purposes of God. We get truths and revelation—the best being through Scriptures and Jesus' living example for us—but the rest will seem, well, senseless.

There is a gap between what we humans can know and what God knows. It is what I call the "illogical gap." Logic as we perceive it ceases to exist when we step into the realm of divine thought. That gap causes some to exclaim, "Believing in a god is not logical; therefore, God does not exist." Others will say, "Religion is the opiate of the people," dismissing the concept of a god completely. The very fact that "God is illogical" reassures me. I would hate to worship a god equal to my intelligence!

"When, by the reception of the Holy Spirit, I begin to realize that God knows all the deepest possibilities there are in me, knows all the eccentricities of my being, I find that the mystery of myself is solved by this besetting God."

Oswald Chambers

I love reading the amazing and highly complex facts about our universe. In the book *Beyond the Cosmos,* Dr. Hugh Ross explains how using new discoveries in physics and astronomy depict a God who exists in scientifically provable dimensions.

The space-time theorem of general relativity establishes not only the Creator's extra time dimension(s) or their equivalent, but also His capacity to operate in all the space dimensions the universe has ever possessed (or their equivalent). What follows, then, from string theory and from all these recent findings in particle physics and astrophysics, is that God must be operating in a *minimum* of eleven dimensions of space and time (or their practical equivalent).[3]

Simply put, this means that people who are smarter than I'll ever want to be in physics and astrophysics have scientifically discovered that God exists in dimensions that we can never fathom. If we live in only four dimensions, there is little chance we can even begin to comprehend a greater being that exists in at least eleven dimensions. There is an obvious gap (scientifically proven) between what God *knows* and what we can comprehend.

God will never make complete sense to our earthly understanding. His mind and reasoning will forever supersede ours. Even our vocabulary is too limited to accommodate the universe or its Creator. We must learn to trust God regardless of how we think or feel. This is what we call faith. Faith is not some mystical loophole for us to excuse the inability to understand. Instead it is the full acceptance of incomprehensive things that do exist, "the evidence of things not seen" (Heb. 11:1 KJV).

Frederick Buechner accomplishes artistically what Hugh Ross does scientifically to describe the near-impossibility of trying to put God into finite, four-dimensional interpretation:

> Words after all were invented to deal with a world of space and time, where as by definition God exists beyond such categories altogether. To try to talk about God in terms of time and space, which are the only terms we know, is like a man who has been blind from birth trying to talk about colors in terms of sound and touch, which are the only terms he knows. . . .
>
> The blind man says perhaps that a sunrise is like the sound of trumpets in a great cathedral or like the way the damp grass feels to your bare feet in the summertime. We say of God that He is like a father or a king or that when He draws near to us it is the way a man feels when he is plowing a field and suddenly uncovers a rich treasure so that in this joy he goes and sells all that he has in order to buy that field. These are useful as suggestions of the reality that they point to, but needless to say they are not the reality itself.[4]

As I've traveled this nation and globe, I've had the opportunity to define why we can't understand. Humorously it seems I've become an expert in explaining why you can't explain. What people appreciate most is knowing that they are not alone in their limited grasp of who God is. Not only is it okay that people don't understand this mighty God, but it may in fact be a sign that they are healthy and normal, because they too have unanswerable questions.

Our pursuit of fairness is not an easy one to relinquish. Since we agree that we are finite beings, and are subject to a greater Creator, there must be a system of logic to fairness that also supersedes ours. We can never understand all things. So we can never understand what is "fair" according to God's divine knowledge. Instead we must hold fast to what God has revealed to us.

Radical Unfairness

Knowing that humanity would not be able to grasp his vast greatness, God came to us in the form of man to show us how to truly live. He made himself known through the life of his Son. This was perhaps the most unfair move God could have made. It wasn't "fair" for Jesus to have to leave his throne in heaven. And if that wasn't unfair enough, Jesus took all our sin upon himself. He took our punishment. Then he forgave—the ultimate unfair act. No, God was not fair.

Take another look at the Beatitudes in Matthew, chapter 5. When Jesus instructed those whose cloak had been stolen to give away their tunic as well, it was like saying, don't just give up your house, throw in your Jeep as well! No, Jesus was not fair as we define it. Jesus was more interested in loving than keeping score. He left no room for jealousy or bitterness to grow. Jesus went beyond the justice that was spelled out in the Law of Moses.

The knowledge and justice of Christ so far exceeds ours that it makes our definitions seem petty. Jesus knows our heart's cry for the true homeland where life is no longer difficult and imbalanced. So he challenges us all to a life of radical unfairness—in love.

Jesus is not concerned that all things be equal but rather that all should be free. This freedom is received only through communion with his Holy Spirit. The conduit that transmits this spiritual union is our faith.

Faith is a word related to trust. It enables us to lean on the goodness of an unfathomable God. (Granted it may often feel like falling.) Although we can't see through our limited vision of fairness, we trust in God's goodness. This trust in the unseen, our faith, is the key that opens the door to the sanctuary of contentment. When our spirits are quieted, we can then begin to grasp our destiny.

> When my heart was grieved
> And my spirit embittered,
> I was senseless and ignorant;
> I was like a beast before you.
> Yet I am always with you;

You hold me by my right hand.
You guide me with your counsel,
And afterward you will take me into glory.
Whom have I in heaven but you?
And earth has nothing I desire besides you.
My flesh and my heart may fail,
But God is the strength of my heart
And my portion forever.

Psalm 73:21–26

Remember my son Luc running up the stairs in a cloud of glitter and fairy dust? Like the psalmist, he yearned for the protection of his mother away from the competitive demands of the other children. He trusted that she knew what was fair. Like Luc, we can trust God's fairness. Rather than treating everyone the same, God asks us to trust in his impartial, unbiased, objective, honorable love.

When the rungs of the ladder break on the corporate climb, or you finally start winning the game just as someone changes the rules; when you finally accrue stock and the market crashes, the place to come back to is God, who holds a different plumb line of justice. *To whom can I turn but you? When it comes down to it, this world has nothing I desire. I want you. You, God, alone are the strength of my heart.*

What good is God in the midst of an unfair world? He met unfairness head-on through the life of Jesus. His definition of fairness reaches so much farther than ours that he challenges us to consider radical love instead. We can trust God, who knows our deepest desires more fully even than we do. We can be assured that, although we don't have the justice we desire in this unbalanced world, God is truly just and fair in his nature. Like a parent who embraces us during our cries of "Unfair!" God holds us in his steadfast love. We rest knowing that he will make everything turn out right.

Father,
I abandon myself into your hands;
do with me what you will.
Whatever you may do, I thank you:

I am ready for all, I accept all.
Let only your will be done in me,
and in all your creatures.
I wish no more than this, O Lord.
Into your hands I commend my soul;
I offer it to you with all the love of my heart,
for I love you Lord, and so need to give myself,
to surrender myself into your hands, without reserve
and with boundless confidence, for you are my Father.

That is how to pray when you are suffering. That is how to believe in God.[5]

9

Where Do You Go to Find God?

The chief trouble with the church is that you and I are in it.

Charles H. Heimsath

Where do you go to find God? Why, the answer seems obvious—the church of course!

I hated the church. It's true. I have to confess that I've been guilty of hateful prejudice toward those who call themselves Christians.

How can that be when I claim to be one? I've struggled with this too. Oh how merciless the struggle! It wasn't until I was grown that I discovered that like a foster child who never knows which set of parents she will get next or where her bed will be or what kind of siblings she might live with, church was the same for me. Some experiences were warm and nurturing while others were abusive, filled with bitterness and volatile people. And one never knew when the tide would turn.[1]

Why would we ask such a question if God is everywhere, if he is the life that flows in and through all of nature and humanity bringing peace and unity—the Great Spirit in the sky? "Where do you go to find God?" may seem to beg the question. Though God's signature marks his handiwork in both nature and humanity, he laid out a plan for us to gather together to fully experience his presence.

This chapter touches a very tender spot for me as I join hundreds of others who struggle living in and around the church. In chapter 8 we discussed unfairness and found that ultimately we trust God because he is good and his love for us supersedes any of our life circumstances. But can we trust the institution of the church, given to us to represent God and his love for his people? Many younger people are opting out, but not without great sacrifice. Do they know what they are missing?

The sanctuary is to be a place of refuge—the safe place to which we come to encounter God and his glory, to pray and confess our sin and look for a new start as followers of Jesus Christ. Church is where a child kneels as a hand is placed gently on her brow while receiving a blessing—words to remind her of who she is—the beloved child of God. We come to the church for our most precious rites of passage and rituals: birth, marriage, seeking comfort in times of suffering, and death. The church is to be a safe haven for little children, the elderly, and those who are hungry.

Though God has an intimate, private relationship with us, we are created to live in community. God's embrace is found through his church. Unfortunately these extended hands can also cause deep and searing pain. "When our trust is violated by those who have been given society's respect for their special role as spiritual caretakers, . . . the pain, injury and disillusionment can be devastating."[2]

The Love of Ruling

While she was pregnant, my late wife and I told our pastor of her HIV infection during our interview for the position of youth pastor. "Every day, our lives are in the hand of God," he responded. "I think we should trust God." I loved my pastor for that tender response.

We accepted the position of youth pastor and enjoyed marvelous ministry in a healthy church. After many conferences with AIDS specialists, we practiced every precaution, although we knew there was no chance of spreading HIV to others. We felt there was no reason to share our medical situation. Only the senior pastor, my wife, and I knew of Evon's infection. Besides, we thought, if God healed Evon, the point was moot. We were hesitant about making our situation public knowledge.

In time, my wife delivered our little girl Ashli. Six months later, confirmation came that our daughter was an "AIDS baby." We began to pray for healing. Miracles didn't seem to come. When Ashli neared one year of age, she had regressed neurologically. As her lack of motor skills and balance became more obvious, we found ourselves lying to people who asked about her development or health. I finally called our senior pastor to discuss our options.

"Pastor," I said on the phone, "I want to share our situation with the church."

He didn't want this to be public. I believe he was concerned about public reaction. I finally shared with him my desire for community prayer. "Pastor," I pleaded, "there are churches and prayer groups all over this country praying for us and Ashli. I want our own church to pray for her. Please let me share so the elders can pray for her."

He conceded. The following Sunday during both services, I sat on the platform as he shared about the medical conditions of HIV in our country. He then shared how a couple on staff had this infection. He explained how Evon had contracted the virus through an infected blood transfusion. The fact that Ashli had contracted the virus through birth was also disclosed.

At the end of each service, 90 percent of those attending that day found their way to hug Evon and me and to reaffirm their friendship, love, and prayer. Another 5 percent sat frozen, unavailable—unable to move. The remaining people—we learned later—didn't like this situation at all.

The following Thursday I got a visit from the pastor at my home. "I know Evon is planning to attend the women's retreat," he said. "I'm here to request that she choose to room alone."

He continued with other issues. "As for the kitchens and nurseries, we don't want Evon or Ashli in them." Continued explanation followed about concerns regarding viruses that might possibly be spread from my girls to elderly or pregnant women. He asked about our teen housekeeper and asked me not to let her clean any toilets or other such areas. Although I explained that we had never placed her or any other individual in danger, the church's quarantines remained firm.

Before he left our home, he shared a Scripture with me. "Doug, perfect love casts out all fear. I'm asking you to love these people enough to cast away all fear. If you love them, you will not put them in situations where they will experience fearful concerns. Love them enough to separate yourself from them." He had twisted the Word of God and I knew it.

I was outraged. Inexperienced in ministry, I didn't know how to respond. So I didn't . . . right then.

> "A church is a hospital for sinners, not a museum for saints."
>
> L. L. Nash

Soon I had experts in the field of church AIDS policies attend our church and address the congregation, but the attitudes never changed. I placed the names and phone numbers of America's top infectious disease specialists on the desk of the senior pastor and children's pastor. If anyone from the church ever called, I never knew about it. Certainly there was no change in the policy or treatment of my family. Nothing I could do would abate the church's fears.

Finally, three months prior to Ashli's death, we were removed from our position. "God told us you need to go." We were asked not to attend the church any longer. Because of our recent move to that area, the only friends we had in Denver were the people in that church.

We left. Alone.

Stories such as this are tragic. They may be unique, but they are not without company. You most likely have a narrative to share too. In Psalm 142, David writes his story while hiding in a cave. David is being pursued and attacked by those he once trusted. It seems no one is concerned for him as his spirit grows faint. Only God knows David's path, so he feels confident in pouring out his complaints to God. He writes:

> I cry aloud to the LORD;
>> I lift up my voice to the LORD for mercy.
> I pour out my complaint before him;
>> before him I tell my trouble. . . .
> In the path where I walk
>> men have hidden a snare for me.
> Look to my right and see;
>> no one is concerned for me.
> I have no refuge;
>> no one cares for my life.
>
> verses 1–4

The psalmist knows he cannot endure his desperation alone—he is suffering and cannot help himself in the impending solitude. David is also a part of a covenantal family, and his pleas come from within that relationship. Like the scores of people I can name, David knew what it was like to have an entire assembly filled with people concerned for no one but themselves. Searching for connection, camaraderie, and communion, David found only despair.

Please understand, the purpose of this chapter is not to offend, defend, or define the church. My desire is that you will be surprised and delighted to discover God in the obscure and ordinary lives of those with whom you live and worship; where you are healed and transformed by God's love in daily living as you serve one another in a community of devoted friends. The world should recognize we are Christians by our love for one another. The difficulty of this discussion is keeping balance. We can't simply rail against the organization known as church. God gave us this plan for a purpose. The challenge is to allow our definitions to change. Who defined the church as a bunch of separatists who gather under a steeple?

What Do You Mean Church Begins at 10:00 A.M.?

The idea of *minyan* is central to the spiritual life of Jewish people. While anyone can pray at any time, before an official prayer service can be held there must be at least ten men present. This group of ten men is called a *minyan*. It was stated in the Law that whenever ten adult men were gathered together in the name of God, the Immanent God himself would actually be present in the room with them. Any room then became consecrated ground, a holy place where men could perform their religious rituals and worship God.[3]

> "Love cannot remain by itself, it has no meaning. Love has to be put into action and that action is service."
>
> Mother Teresa

But Jesus refuted the old law by saying, "For where two or three are gathered in my name, there am I in the midst of them" (Matt. 18:20 RSV). Jesus illustrates here that through his Spirit all believers are connected. It only takes a gathering of two to create the church. With his spirit flowing between us, the relationship is formed. The church is established by this connection alone. The *minyan* is no longer required!

Remember the hippie communes in the sixties and early seventies? Well, take out the drugs and sex, and you've got a fairly good idea of how the church looked in the beginning. The Book of Acts tells how the early church grew as little clusters or communes in which everyone shared. A utopian state of harmony was depicted in those first days of the Christian community, although they were not yet called "Christians." Many of these groups prospered. They made collective decisions and enjoyed common ownership of goods, making the early Christians in Jerusalem a practical model for the kibbutz.[4]

Happy churches today live and share life as an extended family would around a table. We use the metaphor of coming to "the table" to share communion—too bad it often remains just a metaphor.

Why is it that as soon as troubles arise, we snap into an organizational hierarchy to resolve these intimate relational problems? Sometimes a system or process is necessary, but only when we can't resolve our differences and concerns personally. We first need to hug, pray, forgive, and bless one another. And when "family members" need to live in another house for a while, they should receive a parting kiss of blessing on their foreheads.

Whose Idea Was This?

The Son of God walked on this earth and visited the Jewish temples. A devout Jew himself, he worshiped the Creator there. However, he never aligned himself with their legalistic posture or formal structure. In fact, most of his conflict was with those in religious power. "In the gospel accounts, Jesus took no public stand against slavery, racism, class warfare, state-sponsored terrorism, military occupation, or corruption in government. He spoke not a word against abortion or infanticide, homosexuality or the exploitation of women and children. Of all the social evils of his day, Jesus spoke out against the Pharisees and their spiritual corruption."[5]

> "If your brother sins against you, go and show him his fault, just between the two of you. If he listens to you, you have won your brother over."
>
> Jesus Christ
> Matthew 18:15

If Jesus did not "join the church" established then, where then was the church conceived? Jesus looked at his overbearing and boisterous friend Peter and said, "You are Peter [meaning 'rock'], and on this rock I will build my church" (Matt. 16:18). Does that mean that the church was built upon Peter's new office as saint or pope? No. He had no great status or skill. In fact, he later cursed bitterly, denying that he even knew Christ.

Peter was an ordinary fellow who made big mistakes. We often miss the deep beauty of the resurrected Jesus returning to eat a meal with those who left him to die alone. He ate again with those who betrayed him to reestablish the intimacy of their covenant.

The church, then, is meant to be a place where people intimately relate to one another and share life. As they drink of the same cup together, they taste bitter sorrows and sweet happiness and receive life flowing from God. The church was never meant to be an organization run like a corporate nonprofit business venture.

Corporations are man-made structures with hierarchies symbolized by the skyscrapers that house them. The church, on the other hand, is a living, breathing being. It saddens me to see another great word die at the hands of man's engineering. The word *organization* is a wonderful word for the church because it represents the core of the church as a life-giving organism. It is truly organic. Organic structures have cells, lifeblood, senses, movement. Jesus purposefully taught that the church's structure was to be different from all others. It is not a political system or any other drywalled structure described by a flowchart. The church is the body of Christ.

> "One hundred religious persons knit into a unity by careful organization do not constitute a church any more than eleven dead men make a football team."
>
> A. W. Tozer

Jesus once looked at the Jewish temple and commented that if it were to be torn down, he would rebuild it in three days. Those who heard him laughed aloud at this comment! It had taken scores of years to build their place of worship. Jesus, however, was not speaking of a literal temple. In his death and resurrection, a process that took three days, Jesus provided new life for us. He rebuilt the temple by establishing a new paradigm—a body. We now enter the doors of the sanctuary as we embrace Jesus and those around us. It is this community that Jesus brought into existence.

I chuckle at the truth of Henri Nouwen's words when he said that we don't get to choose our community but rather we usually live with those who are typically not ones we would even like. Many ex-churchgoers are critical about how they just didn't mix well with "those people." We tend to approach the church full of demands and expectations—like many singles I know who are approaching age thirty or forty without a mate because their list of requirements either describe a fantasy figure or Jesus himself!

Whenever I get really discouraged with church, I revisit a sage of the faith who sets my perspective right again. I pick up the book *Life Together* written by Dietrich Bonhoeffer, who writes about the extravagant luxury of living in Christian community. Imprisoned by the Gestapo in 1945, Bonhoeffer wrote while in solitary confinement awaiting his execution. He knew firsthand that our shared *experiences* aren't strong enough to hold us together; rather our community is found in Jesus only.

There is probably no Christian to whom God has not given the uplifting *experience* of genuine Christian community at least once in his life. But in this world such experiences can be no more than a gracious extra beyond the daily bread of Christian community life. We have no claim on such experiences, and we do not live with other Christians for the sake of acquiring them.[6]

In other words, it is not a warm fuzzy experience or our love for the same style of music or Sunday school curriculum that holds us together. As Bonhoeffer reiterates, "We are bound together by faith, not by experience . . . for Jesus Christ alone is our unity. 'He is our peace.' Through Him alone we have access to one another, joy in one another, and fellowship with one another. Our community consists solely in what Christ has done for both of us. . . . Christian brotherhood is not an ideal, but a divine reality."[7]

Yes, Jesus created the church himself. As the Creator, God rarely misses in his fashion of something beautiful.

> "He who loves his dream of a community more than the Christian community itself becomes a destroyer of the latter, even though his personal intentions may be ever so honest and earnest and sacrificial."
>
> Dietrich Bonhoeffer

In Whose Name?

Recently, I traveled with a group of teens and adults to the inner city of Belfast, Northern Ireland. If you watch the news, you know of the continual unrest and violence that occurs there, an unrest that has resided in Ireland for hundreds of years. The Catholics and Protestants have been warring with each other for generations. The ugliness and hatred runs deep. It is obvious that the institutionalism of these religions has done nothing to promote harmony. In fact, the corporate structuring has developed war machines.

We stayed in the Shankill area—in the heart of Protestant activism. What amazed me wasn't just their hatred for the Catholics; it was that the Protestants have divided among themselves and they too fight for territory and recognition. Drug lords and criminals direct the activities, raising money for their group. They are Protestant only by ancestral endowment. Rather than marching in cadences echoing their passion for God, they march in organizational hatred.

Jonny Caldwell, a friend of mine in Belfast who hosted us, has a wonderful ministry in that area. The director of Rock Belfast, he has begun reaching the children to present a gospel of communion, not community division. Through Pastor Jon Marx and the team from Living Hope Church in Chicago, they built a climbing gym in an abandoned church building. I watched as he invited schoolchildren to come to the gym and climb, using the ropes course as a powerful metaphor of working together. Schoolteachers stood in amazement as children from differing neighborhoods who'd been taught to hate one another clung trustfully to each other's clothing in the low-ropes challenge course. These Irish children, who daily learn proud defiance, humbly trusted an American holding their rope as they climbed twenty feet above him.

The institutional church has failed those in Belfast. Its message rots in the children even today. I love how Jonny delivers the concept of what the church is supposed to be to his community.[8] Jonny and his wife, Sharon, know the church as community and bring the life and service of that community to those whom they touch.

A Body Conflicted

Many dried trails of blood stain the front steps of our church buildings. To those wounded that have vowed never to darken a church's door again, I ask you for another chance. Few know the dark side better than you. Today, grab my hand; together let's bring healing back into the community God intended for good. Before others experience the same pain you have, let's move again toward building a community of healing. You and I together are the church.

Can we reclaim the invitation of Jesus and the meaning behind his words? Yes. Our hope is found in God's commitment to his covenant. "But how can we succeed?" you ask.

> "Persecution has not crushed the church; power has not beaten it back; time has not abated its forces; and what is most wonderful of all, the abuses of its friends have not shaken its stability."
>
> Horace Bushnell

Like Gandhi, we sit down. Like Jesus, we not only sit down in the face of resistance, we eat and commune with him and those he has given us as community. God, the great host, provides a place of sanctuary where we can be vulnerable, where we can eat and rest. "You prepare a table before me in the presence of my enemies" (Ps. 23:5).

Having had one local church brutally attack my work as a minister, my integrity, and the health of my family, I could hate the church as a whole. And at times, I honestly wrestle with my strong emotions toward the church. But I've found the rich blessing of those who've also tasted the pain and yet extend their life to me in trust and service regardless. *The church is only brutal as we give rise to the evil of man in our relationships.* If you too have been wounded, join me today. Let us sit down and begin the healing.

Come to the Table

Growing up in church, I learned the joy of potluck suppers. After the morning church service, we would all go out to a beautiful meadow near a river or a grove of stately trees and stay all day. No one person was the host, and we all brought bits of the bounty God had blessed us with to share. Little did I know then how these picnics were communion in the truest sense of the word.

At potlucks, the youngest children and elderly were always served first, and everyone had plenty. We all helped set up, and we all rested, laughed, sang, and cleaned up together. You see, true service is not a relationship between an expert and a problem; it is far more genuine than that. It is a relationship between people who bring the full resources of their combined humanity to the table and share them generously. Service goes beyond expertise. Community life is like sharing a potluck picnic.

I am reminded of the story of King David's love for his friend Jonathan and the covenant made between them. Years later, after Jonathan had been killed in battle, David discovered that a crippled son of his dear friend was still living. Overwhelmed with great love, David sent for Mephibosheth, inviting him to live in the safety of the palace and to enjoy king's food at David's table. David's invitation was not based out of pity on Mephibosheth's crippled legs and not because Mephibosheth earned a spot at the table. David loved this man simply because of a covenant of love that had been made long before between him and Jonathan. This is the lifeblood of the love that holds the true church together.

> "Love is not a clinging to one another in fear of an oncoming disaster but an encounter in a freedom that allows for the creation of new life."
>
> Henri J. M. Nouwen

Like the covenant that continued with King David and Mephibosheth, we are to love others with the lasting covenant of love shown to us. We must find new ways in our culture to extend the invitation we've been given to come to the table.

We have hope. We the church are the presence of God, providing sanctuary in the world today. With such great potential for good or evil, we must engage wholly and breathe the presence of Christ into others. The responsibility is a heavy one because we are ordinary and capable of betraying him as Peter did. What then? "He has showed you, O man, what is good. And what does the Lord require of you? To act justly and to love mercy and to walk humbly with your God" (Micah 6:8). This is God's design for us.

To fully engage, we must hope again. We also must forgive and release others from liability for the pain we've experienced in the church. This is no easy task! Hugh Prather, in his work *The Quiet Answer,* speaks from a heart of honest humility. His desire is pure and truthful. He begins by confessing his pain and his desire to be free. He prays a blessing of God on the perpetrator and then waits for his vision to become a reality. It will take time.

> I release you from my hurt feelings. I free you from my reading of your motives. I withdraw my "justified" outrage. . . . In place of censure, I offer you all of God's deep contentment and peace. I will perceive you singing, with a soft smile of freedom and a glow of rich satisfaction. I bless you. You are a shining member of the Family of God, and I will wait patiently for this truthful vision to come honestly to my mind.[9]

Look again at the initial question. Where do you go to find God? The church, of course. Though nature is a great sanctuary that offers retreat and solitude where we can quietly engage the great Creator, we are designed to reunite and to share life within community. We are not meant to be alone. The gift of the kingdom of God, his presence, is found whenever two or more are gathered together in his name. The Spirit is God with us. The Spirit in the person sitting in the church pew, or the Spirit residing in the lady at the produce aisle, communes with the Spirit that lives within us.

God is good in the context of his people. King David longed to return to the temple for comfort and guidance of the people of God.

> Set me free from my prison
>   that I may praise your name.
> Then the righteous will gather about me
>   because of your goodness to me.
>
> Psalm 142:7

> For God is present in the company of the righteous.
>
> Psalm 14:5

Where do you go to find God? You look to the church. With the Spirit of God breathing through her, we can sense God in her gracious embrace. Certainly God's grace is as amazing as his church is baffling.

> How baffling you are, oh Church, and yet how I love you!
> How you have made me suffer, and yet how much I owe you!
> I should like to see you destroyed, and yet I need your presence.
> You have given me so much scandal and yet you have made
>   me understand sanctity.
> I have nothing in the world more devoted to obscurity, more
>   compromised, more false, and I have touched nothing
>   more pure, more generous, more beautiful. How often I
>   have wanted to shut the doors of my soul in your face, and
>   how often I have prayed to die in the safety of your arms.
> No, I cannot free myself from you, because I am you,
>   although not completely.
> And where should I go?[10]

Part 3

What Good Is God in My Failures?

Our final section moves us closer to home. Having examined the pain that arrives in the things God allows, we found that God was still good. We then struggled with the questions of his goodness when pain invades our lives at the hands of another's choices. Now it gets personal.

When our pain arrives with force because of a choice we ourselves have made, do we ask God for help? Sometimes, it seems, we refuse to call out to him. We deserve what we got, we think. Strangely, however, there is a longing to cry out for help.

In this final section, we move into an understanding of God, who also is very personal. We come to know God as the one who offers forgiveness, who puts together our shattered lives, who offers us a second chance. The Spirit of God can meet us here in a very private way. I encourage you to finish this journey with a tender heart. For that is where you will receive the answers to these, our pressing questions.

10

Why Would God Help If It's My Fault?

Any man may make a mistake; none but a fool will persist in it.

Cicero (106–43 B.C.)

It had been a long week in western Massachusetts. The weather was brisk and cold; the countryside lay blanketed in soft white as far as the eye could see. The month was February and I had been speaking in schools and churches nonstop for eight days. This particular evening I was speaking in a church and had just concluded my message.

While praying with people who had come forward to speak to me, I noticed the form of a huge man waiting near the back door. As people began to disperse, I glanced up to see him marching toward me. Now I'm not usually intimidated by others; I can disarm just about anyone with a smile, but this man was obviously not in the mood for a smile. Above a burly face framed with long hair and a beard that reached the middle of his chest, his dark eyes looked pained. This hulk of a man was about six feet, six

inches tall, probably tipping the scales near three hundred pounds.
He wore a red flannel shirt and jeans with a belt buckle the size
of a salad plate. As his heavy boots clomped toward me, I knew
I'd soon be looking at my reflection in that belt buckle. With steps
that caused the church floor to thunder, he approached the altar.
I swallowed hard and pasted on a concerned smile.

"Mr. Herman, can I talk with you?" he mumbled.

"Certainly," I said, stepping up on the stair of the platform so
I could place my hand on his shoulder. Looking more closely, I
noticed that he had been crying. I was stunned for a moment. It's
not that I've never seen men cry. I've just never seen "Paul Bunyan" cry.

The pause seemed endless, but he finally choked out these
words as I listened intently.

"Mr. Herman, I'm a logger, and several years ago, I went away
on a logging trip. While we were out, we began to party." I nodded in understanding, encouraging him to continue.

"I've never cheated on my wife," he said sharply, stealing a cold
glance into my eyes. "But we did party and use drugs. I did some
heroine." I silently waited.

"Well, we finished our work and came on home. I . . . I didn't
want to tell my wife." He wiped his face with the back of his big
calloused hand. "You know, what they don't know won't hurt
'em. We had one kid at the time and we've had two more. After
the third one, my wife, she began to get real sick. We took her
to the doctor and found out she has AIDS."

He choked on his tears and struggled to get composure. I braced
myself for the expected conclusion.

"We had the kids tested and the younger two are HIV-positive.
Mr. Herman, I have AIDS too. What am I supposed to do?" He
dropped his head and wept openly, his big shoulders shaking
with each sob. I squeezed his shoulder as reassuringly as possible in that tense moment. *What do I say?*

Our meeting took place on a chilly February night in 1992. My
guess is that the lumberjack's wife and younger children are probably dead now. And I'm certain he is battling for his health if he
is still living. I don't want to imagine what his large frame might

look like now. I pray for my Paul Bunyan every time I remember his story.

His honesty caught me by surprise, but his story didn't. I've heard many terribly sad stories of people making wrong choices, and the lasting ripple effect of consequences on those they love. Can you imagine the oldest child of that family, the only one not infected with HIV, at Christmas and other holidays? Most of this child's family is destroyed because of a selfish choice his father made one night. As we discussed in our last section, tragedy that arrives at the hands of others hurts intensely and leaves scars that last a lifetime.

We stiffen and groan at the agony of an innocent child suffering at the hands of adults. I would be filled with rage had I not seen the tear-streaked face of the child's father. The lumberjack's remorse brings new questions to the surface for us to ponder in our final section. If someone hurts you, you at least have the option to rail back at them in retaliation. But when the pain you experience is a direct result of your own choice, where do you turn?

We often feel that we deserve the painful consequences of our wrongdoing, yet we crave reprieve—relief or even pardon from it. I'm certain you can sense the incredible remorse of this dad. Never in his wildest imagination would he have ever dreamed of killing his two youngest children, or his wife, and then orphaning his oldest child. His inner pain must be excruciating.

This is real life. We make a poor choice or a series of wrong choices, and the result builds into a tidal wave sweeping over our lives, so monstrous we cannot outrun it. As we are being swept away in the ugly aftermath, we long to call out for God's help. But we hesitate. Will he respond? Why would God help if it was our fault in the first place? We caused it. We didn't mean for this to happen, but it did. If it's a choice we made, we deserve the repercussions, right? How many times have we heard, "You made your bed, now lie in it"?

Why Not Call?

Although I'll only suggest five, there may be other reasons why we struggle asking for God's help. We are like the little boy that refuses to call for help when he gets stuck in a wrong action. Our failure has shaken us and we want to call, but we don't.

Feeling Insignificant

The first reason we refuse to cry out to God in our failures is that we feel insignificant. *God has such a big world to run and so many more important things than me on his mind,* we reason. Instead we sit in our pain, our esteem shrinking daily.

I spent four weeks in training to be a commercial bank teller at the automotive drive-up at the largest bank in downtown Dallas. I had just completed an additional week of work with a supervisor watching my every move and was now working without supervision. It happened to be a busy Monday, and all my coworkers and I were surrounded by mounds of cash, counting and processing as fast as we could.

A man drove up in my lane wanting a check cashed and a cashier's check cut for the balance. I noticed the check was from one airline, payable to another airline. Somewhat concerned about how to process the check and paperwork, I considered asking my coworkers for advice, but they were all feverishly counting money and waiting on their own customers. I decided to process the request and ask them how to file the paperwork later. Being new, I felt my question was too insignificant. I quickly cut the cashier's check and sent it down to my customer. "Man, that was fast!" was his only reply before he sped away.

When she had a moment to pause, I asked the teller beside me, "Susan, how do you process this?" When she looked at the check and realized that I had sent the cashier's check out, she gasped. The supervisor and department head were brought in immediately, and they nearly fainted. The cashier's check was in the amount of $342,678! I had authorized a check for over a third of a million dollars because I felt too insignificant to call out for help! (It all turned out fine. I didn't go to jail, and I'm not paying it off with book sales.)

Punishment

If our insignificance hasn't hampered us, perhaps our view of the consequence has. The second reason we hesitate to cry out to God is that we believe *we deserve the consequence as punishment* for our choice. For example, if you know you will get burned if you touch the hot coal, why complain when you do? We don't believe God had anything to do with our choice or painful consequence, so why involve him? We think we deserve what we got (especially when our choice has hurt another person) and we refuse to call out to him. Again, we sit in pain.

Too Proud to Admit It

Another reason we remain silent may be *our pride*. I know an individual who is so proud that his pride alone may be the source of his panic and anxiety. Those who meet him would never label him as a "proud man." However, his pride lies in his refusal to admit shortcomings or failure. Even with the results crumbling down around him, he will find a way to shift blame. His pride will not allow him to accept the consequence. And since it's not *his* failure, why should he ask God to help him stop failing? He won't.

Others are proud as well, but they *justify*. I see myself in the mirror on this one! As a child, I justified absolutely everything I did that I knew was wrong. It didn't matter how severe the infraction. I learned that if I was just creative and smart enough, I could justify my action. The trick was to convince my parents. By the time I was finished, I had convinced myself too! It takes a lifetime to conquer this demon! As adults we often justify everything we've done. We have millions of excuses and can create more on demand. If we admit we failed, or stop trying to justify our actions, we are forced to call for help.

Avoidance

Another reason we hesitate to call out for God's help in our own failures is that we want to *avoid any more pain*. One young man in Dallas came up to me and said, "I'm tired of asking God for forgiveness. I know I'll just fail again, and I don't want to be a hypocrite. It hurts too much to say I'm sorry, and it hurts too much to fail again." For Rusty, it is easier to just live as he wants and not even deal with repentance and guilt. He chooses to avoid God, hoping to avoid the pain of failing him.

Teens that I speak with call this "numbing out" or "blanking out." It's as if you emotionally detach yourself from the situation. Adults do it as well in relationships or situations that are emotionally intense and painful. We schedule activities that push back the pain, hoping to avoid it altogether. And in that mode, who yields to the need to cry out to God? He will only make us face it.

Asking for help means that we have to admit failure and say, "I'm sorry." That hurts afresh and causes additional pain. So we "ostrich." Did you know that ostriches actually don't "bury" their heads, they just lay their long scrawny necks down along the ground trying to become invisible to their predator? If you've seen an ostrich, you'll know their biggest end is still pretty visible even when their neck is on the ground—so when we "ostrich," you know which end is sticking up in the air! Unlike the ostrich, we should face our failure head-on, not tail up.

Fear of Rejection

The final reason we don't call out to God is our *fear of rejection*. If you've lived a pretty "good" life, this is probably not one of your greatest concerns with God. But if you've really screwed up, the idea of failing when you've tried so hard to gain approval, the possibility of being ignored or turned away, can be devastating. We question the love or acceptance of God when we feel like a loser. We want to "try hard" not to be rejected, or we refuse to try at all. We refuse to call for God's help. *At least there is no rejection if there's no relationship*, we reason.

The only answer to fear of rejection is its opposite—unconditional acceptance. This means that through Jesus Christ God accepts you and me with no strings attached. Not only did Jesus say, "I will never leave you"; he also promised that he would never "forsake us" (turn us away). When we suffer from feelings of rejection, we fall for the oldest trick in the book—doubting that the reach of God's love includes us.

An Extreme King

Passionate. In every aspect of his life, King David was full of passion.

I imagine David as having a reddish tint to his long, dark curly hair. His big dark eyes twinkled with orneriness and a fire that captured the attention of any audience. You would recognize David's wit and charm in Antonio Banderas's character in the movie *The Mask of Zorro*, or David's zeal and determination in Mel Gibson's character portrayed in the *Lethal Weapon* series. David was a lover and a fighter.

Although he was not a large man, David was in perfect physical shape. His years of wrestling with seven older brothers, camping out for months in the hills, and fighting off predators made him lean and fearless.

In my vivid imagination, I can see young David sword fighting make-believe giants with his staff, his sheep watching attentively. Suddenly a lion's roar startles the shepherd. His heart racing, David turns to see a large cat stalking one of his lambs! Without hesitation, he grabs the stones laid neatly on the ground and with his rod in hand begins running for the lion. Occupied with the kill, the lion is unaware of David's approach. With lightning speed, David slips a stone into his sling and makes a perfect launch at the predator. It crushes into the cat's rib cage, injuring its lungs. Wincing, the lion releases its prey and turns on its attacker. Its powerful jaws are set in a snarl. A second stone careens off the lion's skull. Dazed but still standing, the large cat lets out a roar and then lunges. Lowering his head, David tackles the beast at full tilt. After crushing its rib cage, David knew the feline would lose strength. Using his bare hands, David locks onto the cat's neck from behind. In a cloud of dust, man and beast battle to the death. With one final throw to the ground that snaps its neck, David kills the lion.

As a boy, David defended his flocks against lions, bears, jackals, and other marauders. As king, he became the protector of God's people. His nation would run to follow this wild and zealous king of Israel. Valiant men with dirty, sweat-streaked brows looked at this young king on their battle lines with honor and respect. The look of resolve in his eyes told them their king would fight with and for them. David was neither a coward nor a quitter.

As a man of God, David was also fervent. His songs and dance never showed a hint of inhibition. Even when his own queen despised him for his dance of worship before the ark of the covenant, David brushed her aside. His love for God was so refreshing and genuine that Scripture records him as a "man after God's own heart."

Like many leaders we know, David soon fell to the trappings of luxury, sex, and power. David had been awarded the former king's daughter, Michal. And as was customary in other neighboring countries (though in contradiction to the law of God), David took many wives and concubines as a mark of power and political prowess. With his parlor never lacking for beautiful women, David still was not satisfied. Extreme as a leader and worshiper, David was also headed for extreme failure.

One day, from his lofty perch, he saw a beautiful woman bathing. His passion grew to obsession, and with his power as king, he demanded that the woman be brought to his palace. Being accustomed to getting whatever he wanted, David impulsively laid her down in his bed, knowing Bathsheba was married to one of his devoted military men.

To her dismay, Bathsheba later discovered she was pregnant, and she knew immediately who the father was. Her husband had been out fighting for David at the time of conception. Bathsheba knew she must confront the king. She would be stoned when her pregnancy became public knowledge. She had nowhere else to turn.

I can imagine David's response was gentle but anxious. With a shock of reality, he knew he had made a huge mistake. David, who was such a follower after God's heart, sought God immediately, right? Wrong. Why didn't the king, the "man after God's own heart," call out to his Deliverer? Did he justify? Was he too proud? Did he numb out hoping that he could somehow avoid the pain? Regardless of his reasoning, David chose to disregard his fault and cover it up instead.

David ordered Bathsheba's husband, Uriah, to be brought home, hoping her husband would sleep with her, making the pregnancy look like it was Uriah's. Being a man of honor, however, Uriah refused his own bed while his comrades were still out fighting for the king in the wilderness. Cornered in his own scheme, David became filled with rage. He plotted to have Bathsheba's husband killed on the front lines in battle. Once she was widowed, the king could take Bathsheba for his own, providing the perfect cover-up. Like all his previous others, the scheme worked perfectly . . . or so it seemed.

Yes, David was indeed a man after God's own heart.

God too is passionate. In his holy fury, nothing would suffice for the "apple of his eye," other than an act of perfect love. God loved David so much he would not look away. God's heart was breaking. And David's too would break.

The Heart of a Shepherd

In families of Eastern countries, the youngest boy becomes the shepherd of the sheep. As the older son grows up he begins to help the father with sowing, plowing, and harvesting the crops, so he passes the shepherding tasks down to the younger brother and on down until the youngest of all becomes the family shepherd. This was the custom when Jesse raised his family of eight sons. David was the youngest.[1]

Since the task of shepherding appeared to be forever his—there was no one younger for this hand-me-down—David accepted his job with ease. As a young boy, David would pass the long hours away by singing out on the hills. His sheep were his friends. Like our pets, they had distinct personalities. A shepherd often becomes so acutely aware of each of his sheep that he doesn't even need to count them. He is able to feel the absence of any one of his sheep. When a shepherd of Lebanon was asked once how he could keep track of his sheep if he didn't count, he replied, "If you were to put a cloth over my eyes, and bring me any sheep and only let me put hands on its face, I could tell in a moment if it was mine or not."[2]

David failed as a husband, as a military leader to Uriah, as a king to his nation, and worst of all in his relation with God. His heart had grown hard and cold to all those around him. Only one place remained soft—the heart of a shepherd.

David was indeed a man after God's own heart. God shared David's love for little lambs. He knew David's heart of a shepherd was the only hope for David's repentance. So God sent a prophet named Nathan to share a story with David about a little sheep.

Nathan told of a conflict between a rich man and a poor man. David was beginning to think that he had much more important things to attend to as Nathan spoke of the rich man who had a large number of sheep and cattle. Nathan continued, "The poor man had only one ewe lamb. This poor man had developed such a love for his little lamb that it had become like a daughter to him."

A *lamb?* David's interest was piqued. "A traveler came to the rich man," Nathan said, "but being a cheapskate, the rich man refused to butcher one of his own flock to offer the guest a meal. Instead he stole and butchered the one lamb from the poor man!"

The king fumed as he stood to his feet. "The man who did this deserves to die!" David roared. "Did this man have no pity? He must pay for the lamb four times over!"

With the boldness of God, Nathan said to David, "You *are* the man!" Nathan then declared to David that he knew everything that David had done, including the adultery with Bathsheba and the plot and assassination of Uriah. "I have failed," David finally confessed.

In Psalm 51 we get a glimpse into David's soul at the time of Nathan's confrontation. Listen to his repentant heart.

> Have mercy on me, O God,
>   according to your unfailing love;
> according to your great compassion
>   blot out my transgressions.

Wash away all my iniquity
    and cleanse me from my sin.
For I know my transgressions
    and my sin is always before me.
Against you, you only, have I sinned
    and done what is evil in your sight,
so that you are proved right when you speak
    and justified when you judge.

verses 1–4

Create in me a pure heart, O God,
    and renew a steadfast spirit within me.
Do not cast me from your presence
    or take your Holy Spirit from me.
Restore to me the joy of your salvation
    and grant me a willing spirit, to sustain me.

verses 10–12

No, David never did anything halfway. When David danced, it was a national celebration; when he succeeded, he attained great wealth; when he fought, whole nations were conquered. And when David sinned, he coveted, stole, lied, committed adultery, and murdered—breaking over half of the Ten Commandments. As my wife said to me, "In a matter of years, David committed every sin known to man and to every modern-day soap opera! *Days of Our Lives* would do well to take a script from the king's diary."

In repentance, however, David wept relentlessly and beat his breast before God as devastating consequences came to his house and kingdom. King David called out to his God for forgiveness. While forgiven, his kingdom problems continued to mount. His son's plans to oust his father proved successful—mostly because David would not fight against his own child.

In complete humility, David and his servants left the palace. They left the City of David and followed the water drainage routes, or sewage stream, into the Kidron Valley. There was little pride left. After a brief climb up the Mount of Olives, David again descended amidst hecklers and manipulators of his circumstance. Down he staggered into the wilderness. This wilderness weaved itself throughout his being, making his desolation complete.

Why would God help if it were my fault? David must have wondered.

Finding the Turning Point

There comes a point in our failures when we hit bottom. A friend from childhood called me some time ago and asked me to help his sister. She was living out of her car. She had used up her resources, connections, and worst of all, hope. I connected her to our home church for help and counsel, which she greatly needed and appreciated. Before she hung up the phone, I remember her saying, "Doug, this isn't my life."

> "Notice the difference between what happens when a man says to himself, 'I have failed three times,' and what happens when he says, 'I am a failure.'"
>
> S. I. Hayakawa

I'm glad she willingly accepted help. Like many of us, she failed. It doesn't matter how we got to the bottom. The fact is, when we've failed, we're there. What we do next is vital in determining the path we journey from there.

David found himself with absolutely nothing. This wasn't his life either, and David knew where he needed to turn. Instead of resenting his losses, or escaping into memories of his past—his power as ruler, his vast resources, or the pleasures of luxury and sex—David needed to turn back to God, who had made him king in the first place. With pen in hand, he did just that.

> O God, you are my God,
>   earnestly I seek you;
> my soul thirsts for you,
>   my body longs for you,
> in a dry and weary land
>   where there is no water.
> I have seen you in the sanctuary
>   and beheld your power and your glory.

Because your love is better than life,
   my lips will glorify you.
I will praise you as long as I live,
   and in your name I will lift up my hands.
My soul will be satisfied as with the richest of foods;
   with singing lips my mouth will praise you.
On my bed I remember you;
   I think of you through the watches of the night.
Because you are my help,
   I sing in the shadow of your wings.
My soul clings to you;
   your right hand upholds me.

Psalm 63:1–8

The king will rejoice in God.

verse 11

David's first words reaffirmed his position and that of God's. "O God, you are my God." When David's collapse caused his life to crumble, the first thing he did to begin rebuilding was to worship God and simply let God be God. Realizing there was nothing left within him to hang on to, David, in essence, removed himself from his throne and knelt before the God who had called him to be king.

I too have dropped to my knees in resignation. My own choices in the past have carried great and lasting consequences, which cost me dear friends and threatened my career. I relate to David because I too love recklessly and face danger head-on. I dance, I cry, and I fail. On one occasion I felt completely crushed by my debacle. While I sat with a friend at lunch, I scooted my food around on my plate and considered ending my career as one who speaks and writes about God and purity. My mistake had fully winded me.

"Doug, God can use you greatly even here," this dear friend shared with me. "In fact, God called you to his service knowing

> "It's the nature of God to make something out of nothing; therefore, when anyone is nothing, God may yet make something of him."
>
> Martin Luther

full well, *in advance,* that you would mess up. Don't give up; just let him lead you." It took a while for these words to sink in, and then a flash of insight and warm affirmation flooded my being as we sat across the table at Chili's restaurant. *God called me to himself in advance, knowing I would fail him?* What amazing love to call us even while we were still sinners. How amazing, all the more, to choose us knowing that our sin would surface again and again.

King David also knew this amazing love of God. "It is better than life," he sang. In the lowest point of David's life, he turned to God and found that God had an answer for our question. Why would God help me if it's my fault? Because his love is deeper than any valley we can descend into. He wants us to embrace his love so he can lift us out.

Remember the Shepherd

Many people avoid calling out to God because they want to avoid the pain found in the encounter. Yet when we break an arm, we know we have to have someone set it to ensure healing. A surgeon most certainly will create pain in a heart bypass; in fact, he'll open his patient's chest right down the middle. But the temporary pain encountered weighs little against the joy of life following surgery. God knew this when he allowed David's heart to break.

What good is calling out for God's help when it was your choices that got you into the mess you are in? Well, if you're not at the bottom yet, I can save you some time and agony—there is no other place to turn! When you surrender to the love God offers you, you will find his Spirit filling the innermost core of your being. God did not look away from David's sin. Instead God pulled David's heart back to him. While David was young, God had shaped the shepherd's heart with a tender spot, with a "homing device" of sorts. It brought David full circle, back to the heart of God following the king's failures. We too have been given a homing device—the Holy Spirit.

Mother Frances Dominica gently reminds us:

> We have only to want Him now at this moment—and at any
> moment in our lives—and He is there, wanting us, longing to
> welcome us, to forgive us all that has gone before that has sepa-
> rated us from Him.[3]

Though you will have to face the consequences of your
actions and God's hand may rest heavily upon you as he
reshapes your future, you don't have to continue beating yourself with feelings of insignificance or fear of punishment or
rejection. God judges our actions, but only through his mercy.

In the midst of our imperfections and failures, God expresses
his mercy and goodness. He believes in us enough to choose us
knowing full well that we will fail him. We will fall and he'll help
us to get up again. God does not come in response to the level of
our perfection. It is just a matter of time before, like a sheep, we
will begin to wander. God's coming is bound to his promise, not
because of anything we can do. "God is thrust onward by his love.
. . . He comes even in moments when we have done everything
wrong, when we have done nothing . . . when we have sinned."[4]

Do you doubt the reach of God's love? Like David, remember the heart of the Great Shepherd; let him touch your face.
He will recognize you as his own, even in the dark of night.

My Lord and friend, in the quietness of this hour, I want you.
Although I confess that I often feel like I'm a hopeless case,
I yearn for you to stay with me. I want to walk with you, but I feel so insecure.
I'm afraid of messing up.
Remind me that I can't do anything to make you love me more.
Remind me of my need for grace regardless of whether things are good or bad.
I long "to come into your presence unashamed and to sit under your gaze with-
out blushing."[5]
Amen.

11

How Is Forgiveness Really Possible?

The quality that strikes us when looking into the eyes of a little child is her innocence; her lovely inability to lie or wear a mask or to be anything other than who she is.

Anthony DeMello

The sky was so blue that day, blue as if it had been painted by the hand of the Master himself. And so it had been. A single cloud floated lazily across the horizon, beckoning our eyes to follow its wayward path. Daring our hearts to dream new dreams, to laugh without fear, knowing no sorrow. I could smell every flower—the roses, the violets, the jasmine—mingling into one sweet fragrance of unmitigated wonder.

God walked with us that day. I've never known such joy as walking hand in hand with my Creator, of throwing tiny pebbles into the crystal lake and watching images flow and change across the water's surface and seeing the hope of eternity there. . . .

We were young then, so very young, younger than any man or woman born since.[1]

Loss of Innocence

My memory plays back the sweet evenings of watching my little child after his bath as he would wiggle out of his towel and run in circles giggling, free from diapers and clothes. No shame. No inhibition. I would feign a chase after him, mimicking his laughter. And so God must have gloried in his new creation as they ran and played in those earliest of days.

How we yearn to go there—to escape and be carefree. When we are met with devastation and uncertainty about the future of our homes, our country, and our world, we long for innocence lost. As my children's eyes are drawn to the destruction being broadcast all over television screens, I move to cover their eyes to preserve their naiveté from the obvious rubble and terror left in the wake of a violent scheme. Ultimately we have been betrayed, tricked.

Was God holding back when he asked his children not to taste from the tree of good and evil? I cannot believe anything of the sort, not after having children of my own. Like my desire to keep them from seeing horror in the news, God said, "Do not eat . . ." (see Gen. 2:17). Adam and Eve were younger than any child ever born since. Why? Because nothing—no fear or secret or shame—separated them from one another, their Creator, or the rest of creation. Perfect innocence was all theirs. Can you imagine?

A Surprise Betrayal

"Can I talk to you for a minute, Doug?" asked the pastor.
"Sure!" I replied.

Not only was he the senior pastor of our church, he was my boss. In chapter 9 I shared how a church asked us to leave. "How could they do that?" I've been asked.

You see, this pastor was leaving for another congregation in California. Though we were sorry to see him leave, we eagerly anticipated another chapter under the guidance of a new shepherd.

A standard procedure in that denomination is for all staff members to hand in their resignations when the senior pastor resigns. This provides the newly appointed senior pastor the opportunity and freedom to build his new staff team by accepting or rejecting the various resignations.

The day after all the staff submitted their resignations, the senior pastor came to my office and asked if he could talk with me. We walked briskly to my office. He closed and locked the door behind him. Turning, he said, "Well, do you want to hear the good news first or the bad news?"

A true realist, I said, "Let's hear the bad news first."

"The board met last night. They accepted your resignation. Your last Sunday is in two weeks."

There was a long pause as his words began to sink in.

"They *accepted* it? Were other staff resignations accepted?" I asked.

"No, just yours," he said with finality.

"Well, why?" I questioned. I thought the resignations were submitted more as a formality for the incoming senior pastor to exercise if needed. "Did I do something wrong? Did I not perform my job well enough?"

"No, Doug. You did fine," he replied.

I quickly asked, "Is this a disciplinary act? Or is there some perceived moral problem?"

"No."

Because my wife, Evon, and our two-year-old were battling the HIV virus, I hesitantly asked, "Is this because of AIDS?"

"No, Doug," he answered.

"Why?" was all I could say.

"Doug, we feel it would be better for you, Evon, and everyone involved if you weren't here."

I leaned back in my chair, realizing a fight would prove futile. After a while I asked, "Then, what's the good news?"

Slapping my desk with his hand as he stood up to leave, he said, "God's still on the throne, brother!"

I sat stunned as he left my office. My hands clenched into fists. Volcanic rage and confusion began to stir within. My eyes burned as the tears refused to come. I wanted to lash out as the reality of the conversation took hold. I loved. I gave freely. I trusted . . . and this is what I get?

I didn't want to fight them; I'd given my heart and soul to this church and the teens. I loved these kids. I nurtured them and worshiped with them. We shared two years of laughter, tears, hard work, and lots of play. If I fought now, it would only destroy what I'd worked so hard to build.

Not only were we removed from our position of employment, we were also instructed not to attend the church any longer. "Your presence would intimidate any new youth minister," they said. So I grabbed my five-year-old son, my terminally ill daughter, and my failing wife and left.

We had left all our friends and family back home to come to Colorado. This church was our new family. Not only was I now without a job and medical coverage, we literally had nowhere to turn.[2]

∾

While reading the ancient text of King David, I am surprised to find words that sound as if I had written them myself. The king of Israel had been betrayed. David's life had been good. He came from a solid family of high repute. He was physically strong, and though he was regarded as the baby of lots of brothers, he had been chosen and anointed by God. Even at a very young age, David was strong and brave. His life had taken a promising turn after he fought and killed the mammoth Goliath. Not only had he freed his people from the terrible threat of the opposing Philistines; the ruling king then gave David his beautiful daughter, Michal, for the feat. Life was good and getting better. David was invited into the king's courts and soon became best friends with the king's son, Jonathan. David's future could not have looked brighter.

All was well, until one day the spear of the current king, Saul, the spear of betrayal, shattered David's world. Becoming insanely jealous of the nation's love and admiration of David,

Saul drove David out of his familiar surroundings and into the wilderness. In his rage and paranoia, he gathered his armies to pursue David mercilessly as if hunting for a wild and dangerous animal.

Though God had anointed David king, David did not yet have the crown. Don't be mistaken; in the years that Saul was still alive, David was never safe. His life was never free of death threats. This tale of an ancient king was not written from the idyllic setting of a guarded castle nestled within the kingdom. David's only sanctuary was in God.

Many of the poems and prayers of David were written while he hid in caves and ravines out in the harsh Judean wilderness. This excerpt was most likely penned after Saul's death, when David once again enjoyed a time of peace and worship in the city. You would think it might reflect the joy of having his adversary removed. It doesn't. Though he was now physically safe, David mourned the betrayal of his once trusted friend and counselor. Here the king reveals his heart's cry:

> If an enemy were insulting me,
>   I could endure it;
> if a foe were raising himself against me,
>   I could hide from him.
> But it is you, a man like myself,
>   my companion, my close friend,
> with whom I once enjoyed sweet fellowship
>   as we walked with the throng at the house of God.
>
> Psalm 55:12–14

The betrayal of David's friend was more painful than being stalked or insulted by an enemy. Unlike the avoidance of physical harm, he could not hide from the pain of his close friend's betrayal.

It's Worth Asking

In our search for goodness and the presence of God in the midst of life, we ask, "What good is God when those I hold most dear—whom I trust—belittle, disappoint, injure, or betray me? Is forgiveness really possible then?"

I purposefully waited to discuss forgiveness until this late in a book about God's goodness. We cannot truly experience God's goodness without knowing his forgiveness. We simply cannot come into the presence of a holy and just God without the cleansing away of our sin. God, who is pure and holy, cannot be intimate with anything other than perfection and holiness or he would no longer be perfect. That is why he sent his Son who was perfect and holy to cleanse us. Forgiveness is like standing under a waterfall and being washed clean of all the grime of life's journey.

Christians believe in the cleansing of Jesus, and after taking a turn under the waterfall of God's goodness, they know it truly is the Good News. In fact, new believers are so refreshed, so filled with delight, they cannot keep it all to themselves. They zealously share with all those around them. They tell about a forgiveness that is so complete that their newfound freedom is like having a heavy burden lifted. The experience is so life changing, it makes one feel innocent and clean—like being born again.

Through this cleansing of forgiveness, our freedom was paid for by the death and resurrection of Jesus Christ. Being familiar with a "give-and-take" approach to life, we feel indebted to him, so we give our lives back to Jesus, feeling obligated to serve him for all he has done. Period. The gospel of Jesus' pardon is truly the best good news we will ever receive.

Something is wrong, however. The paradigm of serving him to somehow *give back* is limited and may in fact miss the core truth of God's heart. He created us to *share* his joy in his creation. This is not a buy/sell agreement but rather an invitation to live life to its very fullest and to extend that invitation to all those around us.

I'm Sorry

Sammy and Tyler are dear friends of my children. They love to play together and do so with great energy. As they tire, they inevitably begin to fight. This too is done with vigor. As parents, we go and tell them to "make up." You've seen this before. With tear-streaked faces, they droop their shoulders and shuffle to one another. "Sorry" is muttered in barely audible tones.

"Say it right," one parent counters. "Sorry!" they say louder, body language unchanged. The parent moves in closer. "Say it like you mean it and give him a hug." Nearly beaten, the children extend their arms and hug. "Sorry, Luc." "Sorry, Sam." Then the hug becomes a tight squeezing match until they begin laughing. Laughter continues for a moment until the squeezing match turns into a fervent competition.

> "Forgiveness is not that stripe which says, 'I will forgive, but not forget.' It is not to bury the hatchet with the handle sticking out of the ground, so you can grasp it the minute you want it."
>
> Dwight Moody

From an early age we are taught to say "I'm sorry" to someone we have offended. Moreover, we are challenged to accept the apologies of one who has offended us. But have we really learned the rich healing of forgiveness? If so, this world would be in much better condition. Forgiveness is real, but not so easy as saying and receiving a simple "I'm sorry."

Anytime petty selfishness, the drive for ambition, or a race for power drives a hatchet between two beings—be it toward God or one another—we are thrown from the soft meadows of Eden into a dry, barren patch of thorns. Only by traveling the treacherous path of forgiveness, cleared by Jesus himself, will we be led back to our heart's true home.

God's Challenge

Two weeks lumbered by after Ashli's death. Bereaved of both daughter and job, Evon and I contemplated, through our pain, beginning a new ministry. Since my vow to Ashli and our experience with our church, I knew I wanted to show churches how it's possible to respond with compassion. While praying about this decision, I sensed the Holy Spirit speaking loudly to my heart. "I will bless you in this ministry, Doug," he seemed to say. "But you first have to forgive the pastors and the church that hurt you."

"No!" I cried. "How could I forgive them? They took away my ministry. They took away my wife's dearest friends and our only sense of support in this city. They rejected us!"

I wrestled with God over this issue for six weeks. During this time of turmoil, I continued to feel the Spirit tugging, "I will bless you if you forgive them." "No way," I would respond firmly.[3]

How vivid are the memories of those six weeks! As God continued to press me to forgive the church that had betrayed me, I would retort to him, "It wasn't my fault! If they hear your voice so clearly, speak to them and have them call me and ask *my* forgiveness."

Why did God want me to forgive? I believe the bitterness in my soul was slowly poisoning me. My heart ventured beyond anger into a cancer called hate. With my attitude like that, God could not commune with me. The fact was, he loved me intensely and he loved them too. He had done his work; now it was up to me. I alone held the power to forgive or not—it was my choice. So God challenged me to "grant a pardon" to that church. Once I had, my heart could be free to connect fully with God's.

> "We all agree that forgiveness is a beautiful idea until we have to practice it."
>
> C. S. Lewis

Pardon Me

Pardon is not a sloppy apology for inconveniencing someone you push over on the way to where you were headed. Though the wrongdoer can request a pardon, it can never be demanded. In lawsuits, when the plaintiff holds the defendant liable for an action, that plaintiff or a supreme authority presiding the case can only grant pardon. To pardon, then, is to excuse an offense without enacting a penalty.[4] I have found that forgiveness is married to pardon.

Forgiveness is also the complete release from liability of all unbalanced offenses. It can strangely free us of our deepest prisons of pain. And it has a deep spiritual dimension also. Forgiveness's essence somehow has roots lodged deep into the inner core of our being—in those same areas where offense and the emotional cancer of bitterness and hatred can reside.

Now, we are not talking about little infractions that irritate us. It is true that the annoyances of life wear us down, and we may need to bundle them up and forgive those things too. But what we are talking about here are wrongs that keep us apart from God and each other—hurts that blister or rob joy out of living.

We've heard the old adage, "Time is the best healer." But there are "deep hurts we never deserved that flow from our dead past into our living present. A friend betrays us; a parent abuses

> There is nothing passive about forgiveness.
>
> Lewis B. Smedes

us; a spouse leaves us in the cold—these hurts do not heal with the coming of the sun."[5] These require much more than simple therapy or self-help courses.

I speak with many well-meaning people who truly desire to make relationships right, but when they are met with anger or contempt or even stubbornness, they easily lose heart. We need a supernatural source of love to empower us and give us the courage needed to pardon the hurt.

Forgiveness is a team effort. We must participate in God's creative work of forgiving. Sir William Temple wrote, "Only one petition in the Lord's Prayer has any condition attached to it. It is the petition for forgiveness." If we expect to be forgiven, we are to forgive. And forgiveness is hard work. It is literally love at work. "We can pardon only to the degree that we love," said Francois Due De la Rochefoucauld.

If you are bristling right now, feeling an emotion much closer to hate than love, take heart. You are actually on your way to being free from the pain you did not deserve.

Hurt

It may seem obvious that we first hurt. But remember from the last chapter the reasons people don't cry out to God. Avoidance, justifying, pride, numbing out. . . . Men tend to grow calloused and walk away, and women more often hide their relational bruises to keep everything happy—wanting to bring equilibrium back to the relationship. Neither of these approaches to hurt brings pardon or unity. They only foster unhealthy relationships.

We experience hurts along a continuum from annoyances to brutality. And it is vitally important to know the difference between forgiveness and passivity. We must be aware of unsafe people who hurt compulsively or because they think we deserve it. Some people hurt others with the spillover of their problems or even with good intentions. Many have been hurt by others' mistakes.[6]

How do you know when forgettable misdemeanors become insufferable felonies that need forgiveness? Lewis Smedes offers an answer:

> You can tell for sure only when you are on the scene. You cannot draw lines for others; you need to feel the difference for yourself. Some people turn all misdemeanors into felonies whenever they are hurt. Other people make themselves passive targets, inviting almost anybody to take a crack at them. But there is a difference, and one of the signs of growing up is the insight you need to tell the difference in the painful pinch of a moment when you are the victim.[7]

We must overcome fear and look our pain square in the eye, whatever the cost, before we can wrestle it to the ground.

Hate

Hate is an awfully strong word, and as a child I was taught that Christians should only use it when referring to Satan and evil. But there may be no other word strong enough to describe our reaction to the deep and unfair pain brought upon by those who wound us wrongfully. "We may feel more of a *passive* hatred—the grain of malice that robs us of energy to wish a person well," but it is still hate.[8]

> "Life lived without forgiveness becomes a prison."
>
> William Arthur Ward

When you hate passively, you lose love's passion to bless. When you hate aggressively, you are driven by a passion to whip someone . . . with hostility. Passive or aggressive, our hate separates us from those we ought to belong to. . . . Hate is the elemental inner violence that drives people apart. It even divides our own souls.[9]

Hate needs healing. Like the malignancy that was growing in my heart toward the church, it is harmful and deadly if allowed to run its course.

Anger is an emotion that raises a red flag that something is wrong. It is a sign that we are alive and well. Hate is a sign that we are sick and need to be healed. It is hate, not anger, that needs healing.

Heal

When we forgive someone for hurting us, we perform spiritual surgery inside our souls—cutting away the wrong and replacing it with blessing. We detach the person from the hurt, from the roots of bitterness that have wound around our soul. After we become free, when the grip of memory is broken, we can then invite the person back into our minds, allowing history to be rewritten.

As we forgive people, we gradually come to see the deeper truth about them, a truth our hate blinds us to, a truth we can see only when we separate them from what they did to us. . . . The truth about those who hurt us is that they are weak, needy, and fallible human beings.[10]

Unlike avoidance of pain, forgiveness is an honest release—we cannot truly forgive without honest judgment, honest pain, honest hate. Releasing others from all liability of their offense is the freedom we seek.

How can you tell when forgiveness is beginning to work? Smedes says, "You will know that forgiveness has begun when you call those who hurt you and feel the power to wish them well. Forgiveness is love's antidote for hate."[11]

Come Together

Restored relationship. I realize that not everyone who is forgiven will live in harmony. Sometimes we must forgive those we will never see again, can't even see, those who have already died, or an attacker whose face we never saw. We are to open the gate of our hearts. For some it may be tearing down a huge block wall.

"We cannot breathe back all the old life; we forgive and reunite on the terms that time and circumstance make available to us."[12] Forgiving is not necessarily understanding the past and its pain. We may never understand until after we have forgiven.

With Others

After a neighbor has offended you or accused you wrongly, you have a choice. You can wait for him to realize his fault and come to you in apology asking for your forgiveness. That wait may be some time! Or you can forgive him without him ever admitting his infraction. *But, Doug, it wasn't my fault!* I know, I too have walked that path. Remember forgiveness is necessary when the pain is undeserved.

When you realize the damage you have caused in the life of another and you move toward them in apology and forgiveness, you anticipate they will appreciate your humility and honesty. At times, however, others will use those moments as an opportunity to open fire on you, searing you with additional blame and fault. Be firm. If they eventually choose to forgive you, humbled by your honesty, the restored relationship can grow. If they refuse, you can hold onto your pardon granted by Christ. You are free regardless of their response.

With Ourselves

Personal failure as we discussed in chapter 10 is devastating. This time, we are our own offender. Forgiving ourselves is perhaps one of the biggest challenges of all. Coming together with ourselves sounds kind of strange. But we often feel split between loving and despising ourselves. To continue beating ourselves for our demise is to hold ourselves liable without any chance of pardon. We need and deserve to be forgiven not only by Christ but from our own judgments as well. "If God forgives us, we must forgive ourselves," says C. S. Lewis.[13]

With God

God has already forgiven us our trespasses. He has made himself available to us, so the coming together is really left up to us. He longs for our relationship, for our intimacy to be restored.

A unique dynamic of God's forgiveness is that he forgives in advance, before we have sinned against him. His forgiveness is based on his eternal grace that extends far beyond our choices in time. By accessing God through his forgiveness to us, we can therefore set our hearts in advance to forgive others who will sin against us. We are to realize that we will be sinned against, and to prepare our hearts in advance to forgive those who do. In that same way, we ask God to forgive us both our current and future sins against him.

Forgiving God

This dynamic is a delicate and complicated one. In fact, I have received some ugly mail in the past when I've spoken on the topic. So listen carefully to what I'm saying before you run this through your theological grid. For Christians, especially, our reaction may automatically be that God cannot be blamed for anything, so he does not need to be forgiven for anything. The Psalms tell us that the Lord is just in all his ways, and kind in all his doing. God never has to say he's sorry. He never sins and therefore never needs forgiveness. Yet we *feel* offended by God. What are we to do?

Originally I thought that I was the only one who had to deal with this intense struggle. Then I discovered that Smedes had written an entire chapter on it! His words are reverent and carefully chosen:

> When it comes to God, our instinctive piety rushes to defend Him against our own complaints. Maybe so. But we should not smother the primal screams of those who feel as if God has left them dangling in the winds of pain. Would it bother God too much if we found our peace by forgiving Him for the wrongs we suffer? What if we found a way to forgive Him without blaming Him? A special sort of forgiving for a special sort of relationship. Would He mind?[14]

You see, we share a relationship with God just as we do with others—only he is perfect. The problem is that illogical gap, our lack of understanding his mind as we've previously discussed. But we still hurt. We still feel anger, and though few of us have the guts to say we've ever hated God, we have certainly turned a cold shoulder and broken our relationship.

The offense has come and we've folded God into the equation. With our backs turned, we've "thrown God out with the bathwater." Unresolved anger brings more separation. Is this needed forgiveness really possible? Yes, it is. And it is necessary for restoration.

Where Can I Turn?

Humanity's love is broken. Even when we desire and strive to love perfectly, we hurt people. "Happily ever after" is a phrase found only in fairy tales. In fact, as I enter new relationships, I often admit that I will disappoint the other person and I apologize right away. I cannot promise that I'll never fail. If I truly love that person, I will do everything in my power not to. But I'll never forget how sad I was when I first discovered that even my best love still hurts and disappoints others. My efforts to love often become movements of pain.

What good is God when someone betrays you and you are asked to forgive? Not only is God the source of our healing and the restorer of broken hearts, he teaches us how to love anew. Ultimately we must turn again and again to the Maker of perfect love to find our way back to wholesome relationships. Only when we experience such love can we turn from damage.

In the midst of the psalmist's deepest relational pain, he knows a place for resolve. He can turn to God's faithful goodness. He turns to God not only for comfort but also for vengeance. "But you, O God, will bring down the wicked . . ." His carefully crafted swords of vicious intent drop unused at the throne of the Almighty. Most assuredly David weighed the costs. Only then would he remind his readers: "Cast your cares on the LORD, and he will sustain you . . ." (Ps. 55:22).

~

Blessed is he
  whose transgressions are forgiven,
  whose sins are covered.
Blessed is the man
  whose sin the LORD does not count against him
  and in whose spirit is no deceit.
When I kept silent,
  my bones wasted away
  through my groaning all day long.
For day and night
  your hand was heavy upon me;
my strength was sapped
  as in the heat of summer.
Then I acknowledged my sin to you
  and did not cover up my iniquity.

> I said, "I will confess
>   my transgressions to the LORD"—
> and you forgave
>   the guilt of my sin.
>
> Psalm 32

Newfound Innocence

Two birds chase and flit across the sky on a bright day. Below is a small pond with hardly a ripple. From a distance, it looks as if someone had cut a strangely shaped mirror and placed it near the meadow's edge. The sky is perfectly reflected, the trees on the bank and clouds in the sky. The reflection is as distinct as reality itself. Like this pond, the human heart is made to reflect the beauty and purity of God. Yet evil has roiled up the waters, and the reflection disappears. How can we regain the perfect reflection?

With the death and resurrection of Jesus, renewed innocence was purchased. Because of this we can glimpse again our heritage, our beginnings, and hope for our future. Forgiveness clears the debris out of the path leading to our pure and holy God.

Some believe the anger of God railed against humanity in such severe force that it drove nails through the hands and feet of Jesus. But nothing could be farther from the truth. "Love, not anger," says Richard Foster, "brought Jesus to the cross. . . . Jesus knew that by His suffering He could actually absorb all the evil of humanity and so heal it, forgive it, redeem it."[15] And he did just that.

The great Creator has breathed a new song over his broken creation. Amid his children hurting and scathing one another, he sang the first stanzas of a freedom song, and invites us to join in.

"Forgiving is love's toughest work, and love's biggest risk. . . . Forgiving seems almost unnatural. Our sense of fairness tells us people should pay for the wrong they do. But forgiving is love's power to break nature's rule," says Lewis B. Smedes.

> We have seen the unpredictable, outrageous, and creative thing we do when we forgive another human being. We reverse the flow of seemingly irreversible history . . . of our own history . . . of our private painful history. We reverse the flow of pain that began in the past when someone hurt us, a flow that filters into our present to wound our memory and poison our future.[16]

I am personally learning to reverse the flow and forgive, not because I want to or because it feels good at the time. No, hate is more instantly gratifying. But I forgive because I've been forgiven. I love because I've been loved. I know that when I only have limited human forgiveness to offer, Jesus promises to do the rest even as my offender(s) in their clumsy gait bump the tender spot of my wounds.

Have you been betrayed? Know this: You will love once more. We can only pardon to the degree we love. Therefore our love needs a depth, width, and length beyond our human capacity to complete such work. Dimensions as these only flow from the Creator of love itself. So we move to love again. And from that same love, we will again risk more betrayal. But to not risk love is to close the door, to bar the gate, and to begin to die.

Love again . . . just once more. Through God's creative Spirit you are offered blessings of peace. Remember the words of King David, whispered to his God. May they remain long after this book is closed. Find rest in God and today embark on the journey of forgiveness.

> But as for me, I trust in you.
>
> King David
> Psalm 55:23d

Almighty and everlasting God,
Only speak to us that we may hear you. Then speak to us again and yet again
so that when in our hearts we answer you by saying no, we may at least know
well to whom we say it, and what it costs us to say it, and what it costs our

brothers, and what it costs you. And at those moments when we say yes to you, forgive our halfheartedness, accept us as we are, work your miracle within us, and of your grace give us strength to follow wherever love may lead. . . .
Remember us. Remember us.
Amen.[17]

12

What Does God Do with All My Shattered Pieces?

Lord, I'm at the end of all my resources.
Child, you're just at the beginning of Mine.

Ruth Harms Calkin

"Just tie a knot in the end of your rope and hang on!" they screamed at me.

I had been hanging there for some time and felt that I could last no longer. It took everything inside me to do what they asked. The knot helped, but the strain of hanging from the rope one-handed while tying the knot with my other arm had weakened me all the more. My solo climb left me stranded. Slightly swaying nine hundred feet above the valley floor, I could feel the sweat rolling off my brow and down my neck. *At least the sweat is staying away from my hands,* I thought to myself.

Several had gathered at the ridge above me to try and help. First they had all grabbed hold of the rope with the intent of pulling me up. But the rope had caught in a haggled old tree some thirty feet above me. One younger man with great muscles considered climbing down to me, but my weight on the rope pressed it into the ground, giving him no slack for a sure grip. The onlookers along the top of the ridge were just passing by that day, and no one had a rope with them. No one had the tools to descend and help me. As a last resort, they began yelling to me various tips for survival. "Help is on the way," they assured me, although I had no idea what kind of help it was.

It was my fault, I guess. I had spent countless hours climbing "Luck's Edge," a sheer wall near the Continental Divide. This time I climbed alone, and now I found my life dangling in peril over Winepress Valley. The safety equipment I counted on had failed, and now I found myself without recourse. I needed someone to save me.

What kind of rescue will come? I wondered.

Help is on the way. Help is on the way. Help is on the way, became my lifeline.

Another stream of sweat poured into my eyes, burning them with the grime from my brow. Then I felt it slip. The knot I had tied began to slide off the end of the rope. Frantically I tried to reposition my hands, but my arms were too weak from hanging and my fingers were paralyzed from my death grip. I squeezed my eyes tightly shut and focused on my grip. Listening to the voices from above coaxing me to "just hang in there," I held on, with all my might. *Help is on the way. Help is on the way.*

I don't know when it happened. My arms had been cramping for some time, and I never realized the exact moment I fell. It wasn't until I sensed the cool breeze blowing up from below that I knew I was falling.

Help is on the way, I thought to myself. *My Rescuer still has time. I haven't crashed yet.* With faith, I could sense God's presence nearby. I closed my eyes tight again and waited for him to swoop in and deliver me from my peril. *He never fails and he always keeps his promises,* I repeated to myself.

In the movies this is where the climber brushes the side of a ledge and grabs hold, saving his life by a millimeter. Or a helicopter hovers near casting a net or a ladder or something. . . . The valley floor was approaching fast. No parachute, no stuntman, no camera crew, just the wind. *Help is on the way. Help is on the way.* The dizzying effect made me hallucinate. Was my Savior near? I could feel him. When would he make his move?

With a deafening sound, I hit the bottom and everything went black. With sudden impact, my life shattered into a million pieces. Dreams and hopes were dashed there on the cold granite floor. My soul lay bleeding and lifeless. I couldn't move. I gasped for air, and I kept swallowing and swallowing. I couldn't see. Was I facing up or down? *Am I dead?* Nothing moved but my pulse. I was still alive but shattered.

> "God creates out of nothing. Therefore until a man is nothing, God can make nothing out of him."
>
> Martin Luther

Help . . . way. I couldn't connect my thought . . . *is . . . the way. Help, help, help.*

~

Thankfully, that was just a bad dream. But in real life, many of us go solo in dangerous situations. There comes a time when we find ourselves, for whatever reason, dangling over a deep valley. Our friends can't help us. They, like the bystanders in my dream, can only offer hollow words with good intent in hopes that we can pull through.

As a child, I remember hearing about God. I was told that God was an eleven-hour, fifty-nine minute, fifty-nine second God. "He may not come when you think he should," chuckled a church elder, "but he always makes it in time."

My life experience seemed to prove otherwise. God didn't come in time. I had "held on" as long as I could, and then I began falling, waiting for my Savior to swoop down and catch me like Superman saving Lois Lane. I prayed even in my rapid descent. Then I hit bottom.

Perhaps you too have hit bottom. You pray for another breath and beg to see clearly again, only to sit up and discover your life scattered in what seems to be millions of broken pieces. *What am I going to do?* Silence. That question was useless. Well then,

What is God going to do with this? Before, I was somebody, but now I'm worthless!

The Village of Tocheleth

Dust blew through the little village of Tocheleth, creating little brown swirls that danced into the corners of the adobelike structures. Harmonizing with the breeze was the staccato rhythm and hum of the handmills of several village women grinding grain. The people were kind and trusting with rarely a crime in their quaint community. It was a hot summer day and the village of Tocheleth had run out of freshwater. The village leadership had agreed that families would have to bring in freshwater from the nearby cities of K'duneuo or Sychar.

> "It appears as if God were sometimes most unnatural; we ask Him to bless our lives and bring benedictions, and what immediately follows turns everything into actual ruin. The reason is that before God can make the heart into a garden of the Lord, He has to plough it, and that will take away a great deal of natural beauty."
>
> Oswald Chambers

Yachal, a little girl in Tocheleth, found herself in the mornings working hard with her mother, Tiquah. They spent many hours cleaning, cooking, and gathering water and food. Papa was a wonderful potter and spent long hours every day in his pottery. "Seber," his friends would say to him, "no one makes pottery in this valley as fine as you!" Papa would just smile. He took great pride in his work and was very picky about the items he displayed for sale in Tocheleth. Everyone who owned a piece of Seber's pottery knew he was proud of his work. Seber's initials and those of his city were on every piece. "S of T."

With a freshwater shortage, Seber and Tiquah agreed to have Yachal travel to K'duneuo to gather the freshwater. With Mama and Papa busy with their own duties, it was the only option for them to get drinking water. Yachal snatched her family's yoke and set off. With the long wooden rod extended across her shoulders and the large empty vessels dangling from each end, Yachal's shadow stretched long and thin, making her dream of being one of the beautiful young women of the village. She straightened her posture, dreaming of how she might look with coins braided across her forehead on her wedding day. As she walked along, Yachal shuffled her feet in a type of dance, singing an old psalm her mother had taught her. "But as for me, I will always have hope; I will praise you more and more . . ."

Soon she entered K'duneuo and came to a vendor. "Excuse me, sir, where can I get freshwater for the people of Tocheleth?" "There is no freshwater here!" barked the old man named Daka. "Run along before I break your yoke." Terrified, Yachal ran through the dark little village, her pots bouncing beside her. Finally, she came to the edge of another town, larger than K'duneuo. This was the city of Sychar and she went to the place of Jacob's well. A man was overseeing the children and women filling their vessels. Only two vessels per household were allowed, so they were cautioned to be careful.

After filling her pots, Yachal steadied herself and lifted them by the yoke onto her shoulders and gingerly turned to go home. After taking just a few steps, her foot came down on a sharp stone and her ankle twisted. In pain, her knee buckled and one of the pots bumped the ground. A large crack severed the vessel and water gushed out. With the yoke now fully out of balance, the other pot came crashing to the ground with much more force. Crack! Water again burst forth, with this pot destroyed, broken in many pieces of different sizes.

Yachal sat down and wept. She didn't care that the water was getting her wet and muddy. She had come all this way and must return with nothing. And now Papa's fine vessels were ruined! Slowly she began gathering up as many of the shards of pottery as she could hold in her little dress. Some pieces had to be left behind, and she began her walk home, the pottery pieces clanking and clacking together in her skirt as she walked.

Arriving home, Yachal entered her home. When Tiquah and Seber saw her dirty tearstained face and the broken shards, her papa raised an eyebrow and Mama gently embraced her. "I'm sorry, Abba," she cried, "I ruined your pots and now they are useless."

Seber just smiled. "Yachal. Come child. Would you do me a favor?" Wiping a dirty tear, she nodded. "Good," he said. "You are a big girl now. Take this *ostraka* (broken piece of pottery) to Joash the baker. He will know what to do with it."

She wrinkled her brow in confusion. "Joash the baker?" she asked.

"He will know what to do with it," Papa reaffirmed. "Use both hands."

Yachal walked out the door and threw a confused but trusting glance over her shoulder to her parents. She arrived at Joash's bakery where the aroma of fresh baked bread filled one's senses. Joash was a large man, his belly rounded like the breads he baked every day. "Yachal! How are you this fine day?" he asked.

"Abba told me to give you this broken shard and you would know what to do with it," she said. She slowly lifted the broken piece of pottery with the handle from the former pot still attached.

Joash smiled, his pudgy face stretched wide and his eyes turned to little creases. "Hold it still, child," he said. Grabbing a pair of long metal tongs, Joash reached into his oven and removed a red-hot ember. He gently placed it on the broken shard. "Take this home to your mama," he said. "She's been waiting for this."

Yachal walked very gently to her home, fascinated by the glimmer of the ember. Entering she saw her parents' warm smiles. Her mother placed the hot ember in the oven and surrounded it with other coals. Then she sat and asked Yachal to sit on her lap.

"You see, Yachal. The pots Abba makes are very useful and are designed with a purpose. But when something happens and the pot breaks, the usefulness only multiplies. With these broken shards, we carry hot embers, or record our thoughts and business notes. In fact, many of my kitchen tools were once larger vessels and platters. You are no longer a little girl who plays all day. Now that you are our big girl, you will learn these things."

Yachal smiled. Leaning her head into Mama's chest, her gaze landed on several clay instruments Mama had neatly stacked near the bread oven. The work of the potter had many uses she had never noticed before.

Back at Jacob's well, a man named Jesus of Nazareth was resting alone after a long, weary journey while his friends went into the village to buy food. A Samaritan woman came to the well to draw cool water from the deep pit. It was midday and the sun's heat was intense. After setting her water jug down carefully where it would not tip, she lifted the veil on her face to wipe her brow. Then she stooped to make sure the rope was securely knotted on her leather bucket that she would lower down to draw water.

"Please give me a drink of water," Jesus said to her (read John 4).

Shocked, the Samaritan woman adjusted her veil back into place. Without turning she knew by his accent this man was obviously a traveling Jew.

"Are you speaking to me?" her voice had an edge of contempt. Jews had no dealings with Samaritans then. Perhaps it was the heat mixed with fatigue that made her spout, "You are a Jew and I am a woman—a Samaritan woman!"

Unmoved by her tone, Jesus answered, "If you knew the gift of God, and who it is who says to you, 'Give me a drink,' you would have asked me instead and I would have given you a drink."

Baffled, the woman turned, making eye contact with the stranger for the first time. His eyes were kind. Her knees buckled and she leaned against the edge of the well.

"But you don't have a rope or a bucket," she said. Gathering her wits she turned back to lower her own. Her voice echoed into the cavern below, "The well is deep; where then do you get that living water . . . ater . . . ater?" She pulled the bucket up. Reaching down, she picked up a broken shard in which to pour this fascinating man a drink of water.

This woman was comfortable with men. She knew that the customs of the day fell away after dark, but here she was with a Jew in broad daylight. She had nothing to lose and it showed in her tone. "You are not greater than our ancestor Jacob who gave us this well, are you? How can you offer better water than he and his sons and his cattle enjoyed?"

She handed Jesus the shard filled with cool water and he drank it all. When she offered him more, he motioned instead for her to get a drink. He knew this woman was as broken as the piece of clay that he held in his hands. Jesus then replied, "People soon become thirsty again after drinking this water. But the water I give them takes away thirst altogether." Her sharp tone was now gone. He was gentle but had spoken with authority. For a moment, she forgot who she was, "Please sir, give me some of that water!"[1]

~

Broken vessels are not useless, they are simply changed in the capacity they are used. Vessels made of clay are especially versatile. Pottery is one of the most durable things man has ever made. Glass flakes away, metals corrode and rust, wood and fabrics are destroyed by dampness and insects. Pottery alone survives.[2]

Do you know what you are made of? I'm not talking about "sugar and spice" or "puppy dogs' tails." Nor am I speaking of integrity or strength. Physically, what are you made of? If you didn't know by now . . . you are made of dirt. (See why I don't write self-help books?) Yeah, you and I are basically big balls of mud. But we are the most amazing dirt-balls on the planet. Interesting, isn't it, that the pottery in our story is made from the same elements as we are? Dirt. Water. A design. A process. A purpose. The only difference is that God breathed life into us. His Spirit gives our pulse its rhythmic dance.[3]

In the story of Yachal, we find the three uses of clay to be similar to our initial design. The clay carried water to thirsty people. Its shards carried fire and were also used to record words. Water, fire, and words; all carried by the clay.

You see, in the Scriptures God is metaphorically described as water, fire, and the Word. In this exciting way we understand that it is our innate design to be those who deliver God to others who need him. As clay, we have never lost our purpose.

If you find yourself on the valley floor broken into pieces, you may think your life is over. In fact it has only begun. With those various pieces, God may be able to use you now more than ever before.

The Great Healers

Humility and brokenness are powerful tools in the hand of God.

It is from the metaphor of clay that I speak of brokenness. That the broken, vulnerable places in my life, the parts that often embarrass me or that I am easily ashamed of serve others best. This redeemed brokenness creates a wholeness that we are humanly incapable of creating or claiming for ourselves.

It's been said that suffering prepares the heart for true compassion. Perhaps the final step in healing is the discovery of this capacity for compassion. Through our brokenness we can offer hope as well as serve others.

Donna said to me the week following the attack on America, "Doug, I am deeply troubled by a nation who joins hands nationwide in a day of mourning and prayer and then goes shopping the next day." Sure our economists are grateful for the little shot in the arm from sales being up. But newscasters broadcast that America went to the malls hoping to regain normalcy. What is wrong with a nation who shops to regain equilibrium, rather than being still long enough to find deep and lasting change?

How many times do we recover from our pain just well enough to "function," then lock our smoky duds and the journey in the closet. Slamming the door, we are ready to be rid of the experience. We just want to be normal again. Little do we know that we are locking up the greatest gift we can offer another—not answers, but rather compassion and empathy. You may never have to speak a word of your story. After enduring a difficult struggle, the fragrance of fire lingers for others to notice.

Whole Brokenness

Instead of discovering wholeness, I find truth most fully when I am embraced in the community of brokenness. Not just brokenness but a redeemed brokenness. I am never whole enough to offer another person wholeness. Perhaps today's contemporary philosophers or spiritual gurus are merely staking a claim that we are not fragments, merely pieces thrown together from the big bang. Maybe they too are trying to make sense about our purpose and meaning in life. Are they merely naming their desire for unity and peace? Maybe we are simply using different semantics, but *one thing is for certain, brokenness alludes to the reality that I cannot live a life of wholeness on my own.* I am in need of God's divine intervention.

If philosophers and the New Age movement err on the side of being too whole, Christians are equally at fault for erring on the side of trying to fix things up. Seeing yourself as a fixer may cause you to see brokenness everywhere, to sit in judgment of life itself. Serving is much different than fixing. But, says Dr. Naomi Remen, "Service is not about fixing life, outwitting life, manipulating life, controlling life, or struggling to gain mastery over life. When we serve, we discover that life is holy."[4]

> "The highest service may be prepared for and done in the humblest surroundings.
>
> "In silence, in waiting, in obscure, unnoticed offices, in years of uneventful, unrecorded duties, the Son of God grew and waxed strong."
>
> Inscription in the
> Stanford University Chapel

Bread and Wine

Look around. Do you see people who are cold and hungry? Have you engaged the eyes of those longing for words that are true and eternal. Do you encounter people who are thirsty for something more?

The metaphor of the Valley of the Winepress at the beginning of this chapter holds significant meaning. Grapes are simply grapes until they are crushed. Of course, if you are a grape, you won't enjoy the crushing. But then, the grape does not realize its grand future! It doesn't know of the aging process and the rich hearty flavor that only time and process can extract from its juices.

You may find yourself crushed on this valley floor. But it is there that God does his best work. In Winepress Valley, you may find new life as you lose your old one.

Jesus said, "I am the fruit of the vine." In that same context he declared, "I am the bread of life, broken for you." Remember the German word *durchleiden* from chapter 3, the word meaning "to know as a result of suffering with your entire being"? Jesus has declared his ability to know us intimately, only because he has fully suffered for us. Through the crushing of Jesus, he pours his life out for us. His brokenness offers to us the Bread of Life that fills our spiritual hunger pains. In essence we will be saved by one whose life was once shattered.

The miracle of our brokenness is that we share in the miracle of the resurrected Christ. Just as Jesus broke the loaves of bread for his disciples, we are bread in the hands of Christ.

As a child I was brought up to believe that because of our fallen human nature, our will was evil. God had to stamp it all out, breaking our will again and again before we could receive his mercy in humility. Only like slaves who have no identity of their own and

> "God can never make us wine if we object to the fingers He uses to crush us with. If God would only use His own fingers and make us broken bread and poured out wine in a special way! But when He uses someone whom we dislike, or some set of circumstances to which we said we would never submit, and makes those the crushers, we object."
>
> Oswald Chambers

no self-pride, and are chained to the master's orders, could we then serve God. How fresh was the message received from Henri Nouwen, who reminded me that we are bread in the hands of Christ. First he chooses us. Then holding us tenderly in his hands, he blesses us. Only after our choosing and being held and blessed does he begin to break us. The breaking is a fluid movement with giving. Jesus breaks and gives, breaks and gives, breaks and gives. We are not broken for a heavenly comedy session or to make us slaves to the will of God. We are broken as part of the ongoing miracle of feeding the multitudes the Bread of Life. Our brokenness is God's gift to a hungry world.

Today you may be lying on the valley floor. Your pulse may be faint. You can sense the Savior is near. Then you hear the footsteps. What good is God when you feel stomped and broken?

He not only provides a miracle of beauty and purpose through each one of us, he offers us as a gift to his hungry and thirsty world.

≈

Remember Yachal? She may have sung a simple song as she sauntered off toward Jacob's well. Here is more of that song.

> But as for me, I will always have hope;
>> I will praise you more and more.
> My mouth will tell of your righteousness,
>> of your salvation all day long,
>> though I know not its measure.
> I will come and proclaim your mighty acts, O Sovereign Lord;
>> I will proclaim your righteousness, yours alone.
> Since my youth, O God, you have taught me,
>> and to this day I declare your marvelous deeds.
> Even when I am old and gray,
>> do not forsake me, O God,
> till I declare your power to the next generation,
>> your might to all who are to come.
> Your righteousness reaches to the skies, O God,
>> you who have done great things.
>> Who, O God, is like you?
> Though you have made me see troubles, many and bitter,
>> you will restore my life again;
> from the depths of the earth
>> you will again bring me up.
> You will increase my honor
>> and comfort me once again.

Psalm 71:14–21

The psalmist knew of the restoration and comfort of our God. As the Potter reshapes your life, you can pray this psalm aloud or sing it over in your mind to a tune of your own.

King David was nearing the end of his life. An old man, he looked back over his years of service and reflected in his final prayer—Psalm 71. His long years of trusting God proved to him again that God was more than faithful. David had been broken and shattered into millions of pieces in his lifetime. In every crushing moment, God would tenderly work to restore David and fulfill his own promises to the king.

What does God do with your shattered pieces? Gently the Savior picks up each and every piece of your life. Not one escapes his sight. Every slivered faction is taken to himself. Never will you be the same again. Your shape may have shattered, but your essence remains. You were pressed and were fired in the furnace of the Great Potter. Though your purpose may be different, your legacy will remain forever as a carrier, the server of the Living Water, Fire, and Eternal Word.

O Potter of heaven,
We lie still and sense the broken shards of our own lives —
our dreams and hopes, our failures and accomplishments, even our family.
Kneel beside us and collect us again.
Into every confused and fractured element,
breathe your life and purpose anew.
If we are to be poured out like wine, crush us thoroughly.
If we are to be bread for our neighbor, break us repeatedly.
Write your words on our hearts and fill us with your fire,
that we may indeed bring good news with impassioned hearts.
Shattered, we lie in wait for your hands.
Amen.

Doug Herman

Conclusion

God of the Second Chance

To take all that we are and have and hand it over to God may
not be easy; But it can be done, and when it is done, the world
has one less candidate for misery.

Paul E. Scherer

I was one of ten students in my class that attended a country
elementary school in south-central Nebraska. Every spring, we
would hop on the school bus and ride to a large high school
track and field. There we would meet several other rival schools
for "field day." We knew the best school would win—ours!

During this exciting day out, we competed in various sport-
ing events. I clearly remember our teachers competing in the
shoe kick competition—and we'd run for cover when high-
heeled pumps flew every which way! Remember those two-inch
spikes with pointed toes? We had some wicked kickers! Though

the competitions included several such sports familiar to us south-central Nebraskans (ha!), I stuck with tradition and competed in the long jump and the fifty-yard dash.

Each year I exercised and ate all I could. With all my daily stretches I was sure that I'd grown, but it always seemed my opponents were bigger than I was. That year all ninety pounds of me felt like a rubber band when I saw some of those other guys. But I was ready! My blood raced with lightning speed as I got into position for the race. As we crouched into the ready pose, the starter would yell, "Set!" Seconds later, he'd pull the trigger. That one word, "Set!" was somehow wired directly to my legs that signaled the message, "Adrenalin Turbo." Tense and quivering, my legs were ready to bolt. I envisioned the dust puffing up behind me like the Roadrunner and Wylie E. Coyote.

"Set!" Suddenly, a large boy to my left raced forward moments before the gun exploded. We all took off as well, but he was already several steps ahead. My heart sunk. *Tweep!* Just then the official blew his whistle. "False start!" he screamed. Grinning smugly, I returned to my starting block. We got a second chance for a fair race.

Throughout this book, we've been wrestling with some hard questions. It's been my joy to walk with you through some pretty gnarly curves on the path toward God's goodness. I admit I have wondered at times if we would find a dimension of divine good in the dark evil that prompted our thoughts. Now as we are nearing the finish line, we've got the wind at our backs and we say with confidence, "God is good."

His goodness spans as wide as his love. Which area of goodness is most profound? Who could possibly say? We each may choose a different aspect of God's character that touches us personally. I have found God's forgiveness to be the apex of my journey with him. The most amazing aspect of his goodness is found while looking out from the mountaintop of forgiveness across the horizon of the future. What brings me hope is that he is the God of the second chance. Similar to that fifty-yard dash, we often feel slighted in life. But God is good in giving us an opportunity to run again. We get a "do-over" with him.

I Will Be Right Back

Paycom St. Louis

231 S Bemiston Ave
Suite 1120 Clayton, MO
63105

📞 877-282-6065

Paycom

100 First St
Suite 315
06

📞 844

EMIUM

iolence

A Fork in the Road

God has provided us with many do-overs, and we've come to one now.

> "God can make you anything you want to be, but you have to put everything in His hands."
>
> Mahalia Jackson

You may have picked up this book for several reasons. As you've read, you may have experienced shock and hurt in response to a God who allowed the earthquake in Lisbon, Portugal, while victims worshiped him in churches. You may have ached with those confused in life's blizzards. Then, you felt your own wounds from others who've betrayed you. You might even find yourself facing God himself with issues to resolve. I hope you didn't stop short of the valley of forgiveness. Our own choices also bring disappointments and brokenness. Did you discover a God who desires to reshape your life from shattered pieces?

Today we are nearing the end of our journey together. The road forks before us. One path leads to the heart of our God. That path will bring its own set of questions, but with them comes healing within the embrace of our Father. The other path leads to continued questions and unresolved pain.

The choice seems like it should be easy—take the path to God! But I too have stood at this fork myself and pondered it for some time. The way is long and to choose is to commit. And again, we find ourselves in the fragile spot of having to trust.

We do not have to be in fantastic shape for this journey. Buechner reminds us that God's Spirit is with us. He will tend to us as we journey. We have told many stories of children depicting their vulnerability, their innocence, and their unwavering trust. Children don't seem at all concerned that their thoughts are simple and unclouded by difficult things.

God as Father

Though King David reached the pinnacle of world power in his time, his heart remained tender like a child's. Here we'll find a brief song that brings us to our final posture with God.

Psalm 131 is a simple but poignant piece that encourages us in times that we don't understand all the great concerns of life or why God does not seem to be meeting our needs. David assures us again that we can trust God and place our hope in him.

> My heart is not proud, O LORD,
>   my eyes are not haughty;
> I do not concern myself with great matters
>   or things too wonderful for me.
> But I have stilled and quieted my soul;
>   like a weaned child with its mother,
>   like a weaned child is my soul within me.
> O Israel, put your hope in the LORD
>   both now and forevermore.
>
> Psalm 131

What powerful imagery and humble confession. David has come full circle and has allowed the brokenness to do its work. "My heart is not proud . . . my eyes are not haughty," he sings. Needless to say, at the time David was writing, he had been through a battle of pride or power. But here David is again tender and pliable in God's hand.

Are we ready to give up our screaming to God for detailed answers to our questions? David sings, "I do not concern myself with great matters or things too wonderful for me." When we cannot comprehend the purposes of the divine mind, we must lean against God's heart. God is good. We can rest allowing him to handle these "great matters" that are too wonderful for us to understand. Even our old friend Job wrote, "Surely I spoke of things I did not understand, things too wonderful for me to know" (Job 42:3b).

The king beautifully depicts a little child with his mother after the toddler has been weaned. Unlike most children in America, those in the Bible and many children of other cultures today nurse until they are two or even three years old. So the child King David describes was fully aware of his presenting situation. A nursing child is accustomed to receiving immediate nourishment and comfort when he comes to his mother's breast. But after he is weaned, he must learn his meal will come later. His contentment now comes from her presence and protection. He will either kick and scream or lean his little head on her bosom—trusting that she will provide for him.

Kay Arthur wrote a study book some years ago on the names and character of God titled *Lord, I Want to Know You*. Here she leads her reader through the many aspects of who God is and the names that represent each one. One study mines the depth of God's character as our parent, the giver and sustainer of life, "El Shaddai."

> The name "El" is one of the oldest and most widely used terms for Deity known to the human race and stands for might or power. "Shaddai." . . . also describes His power; "but it is the power, not of violence, but of all-bountifulness." This is the power that a mother has over the child by providing life and nourishment. The word *Shaddai*, stems from the Hebrew word *Shad*, meaning *breast*. This Divine title means "The Pourer forth" of blessings.[1]

Kay Arthur's story is a powerful one where she describes what this discovery meant to her personally:

> Time and time again I have found Him to be my All-Sufficient God, the unconditional Lover of my soul, my Protector. He held me through the suicide of my first husband. He held me as a single parent when at times I was overwhelmed by loneliness, responsibility, and the need to be held. He has held me through times of great financial need, both personally and in ministry. He held me when the pains of leadership seemed almost overwhelming. He has held me when I have failed. He has held me when I have cried for my children and poured out my doubts about being a good mother. He has held me when I've been afraid and had no more strength, wondering if I would ever make it . . .
> When I have run to Him and dwelt between His shoulders, I have never come away wanting.[2]

In the final verse of Psalm 131, David calls for his nation Israel to put their hope in the Lord. Today, personalize it for yourself. Where else can you place your hope? In the cyclical view of reincarnation, there is little hope. Do you believe that good and evil reside only in the hearts of man and our choice requires us to "get it right"? Looking at newscasts today, I despair in that view. No. "Put your hope in the LORD both now and forevermore," says King David. Only there can we find the blessings of goodness and nourishment we need. Only there are we held by the arms of our Creator, knowing he will never leave us.

Identity Search

Who are you? If I were to sit across from you for lunch and ask you, "Who or what defines you?" could you give me an honest answer that fully satisfies yourself? We as individuals—and as a nation—are in search for our true identity. This is a question of the heart. It cannot be answered by our employers, our spouses, our parents, or our friends.

For our essence to be true in various situations, it must be solid, unchangeable, and based on nonnegotiables. It cannot change.

Dr. Jack Nicholson, a pastoral psychotherapist and director of *SageQuest* in Evergreen, Colorado, has made remarkable discoveries in the area of identity development. In his work with me, I learned the power of finding our true inner identity. He explains that identity becomes conflicted if it is based on our associations or our competence. For example, if someone is overly concerned about where they belong—the country club, a specific neighborhood where they live, a prestigious group, or a church group, for example—they will experience conflict with their true self. A telltale sign is an individual who loves to "name-drop." The acid test is to remove those associations and see what happens. If they have built their identity on these relationships, they will be hollow without them.

When we build our identity on our competence, we are also in trouble. Perhaps we build it on our ability to cook, sell things, speak and write, or even raise good kids. People who struggle with this (like yours truly) are usually highly competitive. However, when these areas of success slip away, our identity goes void and we feel lost.

On your next trip to the nursing home, look into the eyes of those residing there. Many are happy and content. Others are hollow, their identity stripped away. They have lost their associations, and their level of expertise in some ability is vanquished. You see, our identity has to be built on something unchanging. We need a nonnegotiable in our soul so that regardless of the many circumstances in which we find ourselves, we remain sure of who we are.

Whether being stalked by enemies, living in wealth and prosperity, or on his deathbed, David knew his true identity. He reveals it in this psalm. His identity is not as king, nor is it found in his successes establishing the kingdom. It is not as a poet, father, husband, musician, or even a psalmist or worshiper. No, David found his identity based in God himself. As a child quietly leaning on the chest of God, he knew his true self.

God as Son

The story continues. We read in the Book of John written hundreds of years after David, "The disciple whom Jesus loved was reclining next to him . . . leaning back against Jesus" (John 13:23–25 NIV). Here in the story of the Last Supper, the disciples of Jesus were celebrating Passover. As they reclined to eat, as was the custom then, the writer notes that John lays his head against Jesus—literally on the heart of God, on the breast of the Man who was coequal with God the Father. Why is this detail significant? This is not just historical memory, says Brennan Manning, "It can become a personal encounter, radically affecting our understanding of who God is and what our relationship with Jesus is meant to be." Clearly, John was not intimidated by Jesus. He was not afraid of his Lord. Jesus was his close friend.

Brennan Manning continues,

> Fearing that I would miss the divinity of Jesus, I distanced myself from his humanity . . . but as John leans back on the breast of Jesus and listens to the heartbeat of the Great Rabbi,

he comes to know Him in a way that surpasses mere head knowl-edge. In a flash of intuitive understanding, John experiences Jesus as the human face of the God who is love. And in coming to know who the Great Rabbi is, John discovers who *he* is—the disciple Jesus loved. . . .

I believe that the night in the upper room was the defining moment of John's life. Some sixty years after Christ's resurrec-tion, the apostle—like an old gold miner panning the stream of his memories—recalled all that had transpired during his three-year association with Jesus. He made pointed reference to that holy night when it all came together, and he affirmed his core identity with these words: "Peter turned and saw the disciple Jesus loved following them—the one who had leaned on His breast at the supper."[3]

Instead of coming to God only for instant gratification and pro-vision, we must learn to quietly lean our head against the breast of Christ to hear his heart beating our identity . . . then we will never doubt God's provision. We will know it in its fullest form.

The moment you press your ear against the Rabbi's heart, you instantly hear God's footsteps in the distance. I do not know how this happens; it just does. It is then that you experience the bond of infinite tenderness between them (read John 17).

Let the Great Rabbi hold you silently against his heart. In learning who he is, you will discover who you are. And as we listen to his heartbeat (like a weaned child), we will hear his words of assurance, "Shh! Be still; I am here. You belong to me. All is well."

God as Holy Spirit

Our identity is found in the One whose fingerprints match those covering our soul—the Holy Spirit.

Our Capacity

Which serves to a greater capacity, a water pitcher complete and unblemished or one that's been shattered and the shards given to all the villagers? Macrina Wiederkehr reminds us that all too often we fight our imperfections rather than embrace them as part of the process in which we are brought to God. "We are pure capacity for God," she says. Let us not, then, take our littleness lightly. It is a wonderful grace. But at the same time, we must not get trapped in the confines of our littleness but keep pushing on to claim our greatness. Remind yourself often, "I am pure capacity for God."[4]

Do you remember the woman speaking with Jesus at Jacob's well? Scripture reveals that her life was unstable and the men in her life were transient. Though her life seemed barely more than shards of brokenness, Jesus said to her, "Woman, if you knew this gift I have for you." He recognized her capacity to be filled with something *more*. He spoke to her of living water—a water that if drunk, will never leave you thirsty. Jesus himself is that living water, poured into our lives through his Holy Spirit. Are you thirsty? You have the same capacity to be filled as the woman did.

Remember the simple dinner prayer of a child? "God is great. God is good. . . ." It is a simple but powerfully true reminder for us today. God is great. And since he created us in his image, we must settle for nothing less than greatness! It is his design for us. "Becoming great seems a little presumptuous, doesn't it?" you may ask.

In light of America's national events and tragedy, we desire to be a great nation. And a nation can be no greater than her citizens or allies, right? Greatness is achieved by overcoming evil with good . . . only the goodness of God will suffice. "Philip Hallie's studies of cruelty led him to discover that the opposite of cruelty is not liberation from the disparity of power. Rather, he found that the opposite of cruelty is hospitality, a sharing of power."[5] In other words, to be great is to offer goodness back to the world, to hold our piece of clay with a sip of living water out to another.

How glorious it is to see people running to one another and helping in moments of need, and the affirmation of those in countries around the world who join us in our mourning. Our rescue workers and defenders become heroes because they rush to human life to save and protect it. We have incredible capacity as humans, for good or evil. "Whether God weeps at the beauty and potential of our lives at birth or the lost potential of graced moments along the way, I hear that voice urging us to claim our splendor and our glory. 'If you but knew the gift of God . . .'"[6]

Our Declaration

God has given us our identity and reminded us of our birthright. The Psalms act as our declaration, reminding us again and again what gives us our purpose, reminding us of whose we are.

The Psalms have been a wonderful guide giving voice to our deep questions. King David and other writers of the Psalms have allowed us to join our hearts with theirs as we express our deepest hurts. "It is crucial for us to remember that although the Psalms begin with our internal world," advise Allender and Longman, "they don't allow us to dwell there, fixated on our problems and dark emotions. Although they express and minister to our emotional lives, they are not a psychology text. Instead, the Psalter is a book of worship, driving us to God by insisting that we look to Him in the midst of our pain."[7] As the writers of the Psalms struggle to find resolve, they ultimately end in the voices of praise to the great God of the nation of Israel—the same God we worship today. The collection of Psalms was compiled from a long, rich, and varied life of oral tradition in the context of worship calling all God's people to turn to him in our daily celebrations and sufferings. "When we do, we find ourselves and our problems absorbed into His bright glory."[8]

Scarred Past but a Glorious Future

You may be looking at your life and the shattered pieces we described in the last chapter and wonder how you can ever race or love or reach out again. The scars in your life are so deep and tender, you question your future and its hope. Those who have suffered greatly often feel too immobilized by their wounds to live again.

While sitting with my late daughter in her room at the Children's Hospital in Denver, I learned a powerful lesson about scars and our future. Ashli was an "AIDS baby," but since there was no pediatric clinic for HIV patients then, she roomed on the cancer ward or the burn ward.

One day I began discussing with a nurse her work with these children. On the burn ward particularly, I asked about the injuries and what was required for healing. This nurse explained to me that when a child is burned, the child is brought to a room where the burn is first cleaned. The nurses have to scrub away all the damaged skin and any possibility of infection, then they place a healing salve or balm over the wound and cover it with a clean bandage.

In time though, the wound must be cleaned or infection will set in. They must peel this bandage from the wound and scrub the wound clean again. They administer the salve again and put on a new bandage. Again and again, this process is repeated until the healing takes place. Of course this process is extremely painful.

After the nurse shared with me and left to tend to her patients, God stepped up to my spirit and began to whisper. I realized that grief is like that. When tragedy comes and burns us, we want to run and never deal with it again. It is easy to get the initial balm and bandage. But to allow someone to open the sore again is unthinkable; the pain would be immense. So we protectively cover over our old bandages and refuse to allow anyone to touch them.

Pondering this further, I came to understand that the healing comes from the inside-out. As the skin grows again, it forms together and endures the periodic cleaning. There will always be a scar there. But that is intriguing too. You see, scars only show where we've been. They don't represent the life and vitality that lies beneath the wound.

Scarring enables us to continue living. If you have scars in your heart or experience, you will relate. The scars we have show the pain we've had to endure in life.[9] I think of Barbara Bush's snow-white hair. When she was asked why she didn't color her hair, her response was that she had gone gray during the illness and death of a child. There was not a chance she would color her hair now.

My mother has said to me many times, "We can become better or bitter." Scars close our old wounds, allowing us to live again while reminding us that we are survivors. Scars are powerful and intimate reminders of our past. They don't determine our future.

What Does God Want?

"His will is our peace," says Dante. And perhaps that is the expression that best brings into focus our deep dependence on God.[10] He longs for us to come to him. When our souls tremble in the uncertainty and fear of our world, he alone can bring calm. It is you he wants.

> Ever since there have been men,
> man has given himself over to too little joy. . . .
> I should believe only in a God who understood how to dance.
>
> Henri Matisse

Though Henri Matisse needs no introduction as an artist, what he had to say about his art is less well known. Perhaps Matisse would agree with Allender and Longman who say:

> God wants us to adore Him, dance with Him, eat, drink, and sing with Him in the experience of His awesome, glorious love. The mystery of His desire is that an eternal, infinite, holy, and utterly self-fulfilling Being wants us—and He is willing to go to any lengths whatsoever to disrupt, arouse, and stop us from pursuing any lover other than Himself. He is willing to go to the extreme of bearing our anger—and even more, pouring out His anger on His beloved Son, Being of His own Being. Through His unfathomable desire for us and His paradoxical methods of wooing us, He reveals His goodness.[11]

God offers his gift of mercy to us each day. Dare we extend our arms and receive it? "What if my choice is wrong?" some have asked. Our prayers and the Bible, especially the Psalms, lead us to the heart of God, the Source of all healing. They speak of the true healing power that flows beneath the scar allowing the healing to take place. Who could say this isn't God? When we say that the Psalms were formed in Israel's worship, we mean a worship that at that time was the heartbeat of the whole community. They too experienced doubt and fear, but they always came back to the truth.

Israel's worship was like the veins that link the heart with the whole body. Says Claus Westermann, "These prayers became the life-force, which went out from worship into the people's ordinary life and flowed back from that life into worship."[12]

On Your Marks!

> "The Infinite Goodness has such wide arms that He takes whatever turns to Him."
>
> Dante Alighieri

God gives us many "do-overs," and we're facing one now. Our race is not one around neatly marked lanes. It is like a marathon over and through forests and deserts. Though we don't know what lies immediately ahead, we know our beginning as the beloved ones of God; we know the one who runs beside us; and we can be certain of our final destination, the heart of the Great Rabbi, Almighty God.

Which way will you go from here? I encourage you to make an intentional decision to head home to the heart of God. When you choose to walk with me down the path toward God's heart, realize that our lives will be different. Our outlook on life will be changed. How we live and love will be different. In his book *Why, O Lord?* Carlo Carretto warns us that "Love will make demands on us. It will question us from within. It will disturb us. Sadden us. Play havoc with our feelings. Harass us. Reveal our superficialities. But at last it will bring us to the light."[13] And in that light, we will finally be free.

We have ended every chapter with a psalm to pray, a prayer to recite, or a poem to meditate upon. Like a trusting child or the "one Jesus loved," rest your head against the chest of God in worship and be free.

What good is God? He allows us to live again. His goodness knows no bounds.

Final Prayer

O God, our Father, we know that the issues of life and death are in Your hands, and we know that You are loving us with an everlasting love. If it is Your will, grant us to live in happiness and in peace.
In all our undertakings,
Grant us prosperity and good success.
In all our friendships,
Grant us to find our friends faithful and true.
In all bodily things,
Make us fit and healthy,
Able for the work of the day.
In all things of the mind,
Make us calm and serene,
Free from anxiety and worry.
In material things,
Save us from poverty and from want.
In spiritual things,
Save us from doubt and from distrust.
Grant us
In our work satisfaction;
In our study true wisdom;
In our pleasure gladness;
In our love loyalty.

And if misfortune does come to us, grant that any trial may only bring us closer to one another and closer to You; and grant that nothing may shake our certainty that You work all things together for good, and that a Father's hand will never cause His child a needless tear. Hear this our prayer; through Jesus Christ our Lord.
Amen.[14]

Suggested Readings

Chapter 1

Philip Yancey. *Reaching for the Invisible God*. Grand Rapids: Zondervan, 2000.

Chapter 2

Jill Briscoe. *Out of the Storm and into God's Arms: Shelter in Turbulent Times*. Colorado Springs: WaterBrook Press, 2000.

Chapter 3

Joni Eareckson Tada and Steven Estes. *When God Weeps: Why Our Sufferings Matter to the Almighty*. Grand Rapids: Zondervan, 1997.

Chapter 4

Frederick Buechner. *The Hungering Dark*. New York: HarperCollins, 1969.

Chapter 5

Calvin Miller. *Walking with the Saints*. Nashville: Thomas Nelson, 1995.
Henri J. M. Nouwen. *Can You Drink This Cup?* Notre Dame, Ind.: Ave Maria, 1996.

Chapter 6

Dan Allender and Tremper Longman III. *The Cry of the Soul: How Our Emotions Reveal Our Deepest Questions about God.* Colorado Springs: NavPress, 1994.

Chapter 7

Francis Schaeffer. *He Is There and He Is Not Silent.* Wheaton: Tyndale House, 1980.
Chaim Potok. *The Chosen.* New York: Fawcett Crest, 1967.

Chapter 8

Carlo Carretto. *Why, O Lord?* Maryknoll, N.Y.: Orbis Books, 1986.

Chapter 9

Ken Blue. *Healing Spiritual Abuse: How to Break Free from Bad Church Experiences*. Downers Grove, Ill.: InterVarsity Press, 1993.

Chapter 10

John E. Bradshaw. *Healing the Shame That Binds You.* Deerfield Beach, Fla.: Health Communications, Inc., 1988.

Chapter 11

Lewis B. Smedes. *Forgive and Forget: Healing the Hurts We Don't Deserve*. New York: Harper & Row, 1984.

Chapter 12

Henri J. M. Nouwen. *Life of the Beloved*. New York: Crossroad Publishing, 1997.

Conclusion

Steve Fry. *I Am: The Unveiling of God*. Sisters, Oreg.: Multnomah, 2000.

Notes

The Tale of an Ancient King

1. This king's writings and poetry are used throughout this book. Spend a moment with the king.

Introduction

1. Robert Durback, ed., *Seeds of Hope: A Henri Nouwen Reader* (New York: Image Books/Doubleday, 1997), 98.

2. Larry Crabb, "Letter of Introduction," in Doug Herman, *Faith Quake: How to Survive the Aftershocks of Tragedy* (Corsicana, Tex.: Kauffman Burgess Press, 1997).

3. Unlike modern poems, the Psalms were not created in the mind of an individual but were formed by what had happened between this human being and God. The form of the psalm is rooted in this strolling dialogue between God and humanity.

Chapter 1

1. Steve Fry, *I Am: The Unveiling of God* (Sisters, Ore.: Multnomah, 2000), 24.

2. C. S. Lewis, *A Grief Observed* (New York: HarperSan Francisco, 1961), 18.

3. Durback, ed., *Seeds of Hope*, 102.

4. Mary Batchelor, ed., *The Doubleday Prayer Collection* (New York: Doubleday, 1996), xiii.

Because we all know him differently, our prayers are unique. No one shares quite the same relationship with God. But life and its daily challenges bring much in common, so written prayers can reflect shared desires of many hearts, just as great love poetry is timeless as it expresses the feelings of those in love.

5. Brennan Manning, *Abba's Child: The Cry of the Heart for Intimate Belonging* (Colorado Springs: NavPress, 1994), 123.

6. Though many of King David's writings reflect inward and meditative musing, this particular passage was written with the intent to share it with others as a model prayer.

Chapter 2

1. In *The Oxford American Thesaurus,* the word *disaster* is synonymous with *act of God.*

2. A quay was a stretch of paved bank or a solid artificial landing place beside navigable water for convenience in loading and unloading ships. In this affluent port city, this would have been a well-known location of beauty and strength to welcome visitors and Lisbonites as they strolled the river's edge.

3. Rev. Charles Davy, *Modern History Sourcebook, The Earthquake at Lisbon, 1755,* 1.

4. Ibid., 1–2.

5. Ibid.

6. Jan T. Kozak and Charles D. James, *Historical Depictions of the 1755 Lisbon Earthquake,* National Information Service for Earthquake Engineering, 1.

7. Davy, 2.

8. Ibid.

9. Ibid.

10. Henri J. M. Nouwen, in a recorded speech titled "Who Are We?"

11. C. S. Lewis, *The Lion, the Witch, and the Wardrobe* (New York: Collier Books, 1950), 64–65.

12. Ibid., 74–76.

13. Philip Yancey, *Reaching for the Invisible God* (Grand Rapids: Zondervan, 2000), 59.

Chapter 3

1. From "Munster Gesangbuch," 1677, arr. by Richard S. Willis, 1819–1900, "Fairest Lord Jesus!" *Hymns of Glorious Praise* (Springfield, Mo.: Gospel Publishing House, 1969), 34.

2. *Merriam-Webster's Collegiate Dictionary,* 10th ed. (Springfield, Mass.: Merriam-Webster, Inc., 1997), 811.

3. Gordon R. Lewis and Bruce A. Demarest, eds., *Integrative Theology* (Grand Rapids: Zondervan, 1996), 244–45. Some eighteen scholars contributing to an article on this theme add great insight.

4. Ibid., 455.

5. Dan B. Allender and Tremper Longman III, *The Cry of the Soul: How Our Emotions Reveal Our Deepest Questions about God* (Colorado Springs: NavPress, 1994), 30.

6. Lewis, *A Grief Observed,* 45–46.

7. Karl Stern, *The Pillar of Fire* (New Hope, Ky.: Urbi Et Orbi Communications, 2001). In recounting his conversion to Christianity, Stern uses the German term *durchleiden.*

8. Calvin Miller, *Walking with the Saints* (Nashville: Thomas Nelson, 1995), xv.

9. Rachel Naomi Remen, M.D., *My Grandfather's Blessings: Stories of Strength, Refuge, and Belonging* (New York: Riverhead, 2000), 168–69.

10. Remen, *My Grandfather's Blessings,* 175–76.

Chapter 4

1. *Oldtime Nebraska, The Big Brash Blizzard of 1888,* University of Kansas. Web site: http://www.ukans.edu/~kansite/hvn/articles/blizzard.htm.

2. James G. Eastman, *American Life Histories: Manuscripts from the Federal Writers' Project, 1936–1940.* Web site: http://lcweb2.loc.gov/wpa/

3. *"Blizzard of 1888," American Life Histories: Manuscripts from the Federal Writers' Project, 1936–1940.* Web site: http://lcweb2.loc.gov/wpa/ and http://rs6.loc.gov/wpa/17120802.html

4. Joni Eareckson Tada and Steven Estes, *When God Weeps: Why Our Sufferings Matter to the Almighty* (Grand Rapids: Zondervan, 1997), 24–25.

5. J. I. Packer, *Knowing God* (Downers Grove, Ill.: InterVarsity Press, 1993), 14–15.

6. Derek Kidner, *Psalms 73–150, A Commentary* (Leicester, England: InterVarsity Press, 1973), 386.

7. Henri J. M. Nouwen, *A Cry for Mercy: Prayers from the Genesee* (New York: Doubleday, 1983).

Chapter 5

1. Allender and Longman, *The Cry of the Soul*, 20–21.

2. Miller, *Walking with the Saints*, xxxii.

3. Remen, *My Grandfather's Blessings*, 77–78.

4. Frederick Buechner, *The Hungering Dark* (New York: Harper Collins, 1969), 102.

5. Miller, *Walking with the Saints*, xxxii.

6. Adapted from Frederick Buechner's prayers in *The Hungering Dark* (New York: HarperCollins, 1969).

Chapter 6

1. Lewis, *A Grief Observed*, 36.

2. Allender and Longman, *The Cry of the Soul*, 39.

3. Yancey, *Reaching for the Invisible God*, 149.

Chapter 7

1. Yancey, *Reaching for the Invisible God*, 117.

2. Ibid., 116.

3. Henri J. M. Nouwen, *The Way of the Heart* (New York: Ballatine, 1981), 31ff.

4. Ibid.

5. From a speech given by Tony Campolo at a Colorado Prayer Luncheon, 3 May 1996, Denver, Colorado.

6. Here's an example to give you ideas: Imagine smelling the camels. Is it hard to hear the king over the lambs bleating? Does the roasted bull cause your mouth to water or your stomach to turn? Did you see the glimmer in young David's eyes when the giant taunted the armies of the living God? Can you feel the pebbles in your sandals as you follow Jesus to Capernaum while discussing Roman government with Simon the Zealot?

7. Psalm 27:7–14 records the psalmist's determination to seek God's face. His determination is influenced by the knowledge that a divine answer would be an act of graciousness. However, David doesn't want to sound too haughty lest God turn from him in anger. So here is a prayer of determination, modified by humility and a sense of unworthiness. But the psalmist also conveys clearly that there is none other than God

to whom he can turn. His parents have even forsaken him. God functions as a parent to King David, and the prayer is spoken in the intimacy of this relationship.

Chapter 8

1. Philip Yancey, *Disappointment with God* (Grand Rapids: Zondervan, 1988), 186.
2. Herman, *Faith Quake*, 77–79.
3. Hugh Ross, Ph.D., *Beyond the Cosmos* (Colorado Springs: NavPress, 1996), 31–32.
4. Buechner, *The Hungering Dark*, 98.
5. Carlo Carretto, *Why, O Lord?* (Maryknoll, N.Y.: Orbis Books, 1986), as cited in Rueben P. Job and Norman Shawchuck, *A Guide to Prayer for All God's People* (Nashville: Upper Room Books, 1990), 283.

Chapter 9

1. Donna Wallace's personal story.
2. Ronald Enroth, *Recovering from Churches That Abuse* (Grand Rapids: Zondervan, 1994), 16.
3. Remen, *My Grandfather's Blessings,* 364.
4. A kibbutz is a collective farm or settlement in Israel characterized by cooperative ownership and communal organization (from the Hebrew *quibbu*s, meaning "a gathering").
5. Ken Blue, *Healing Spiritual Abuse* (Downers Grove, Ill.: InterVarsity Press, 1993), 18.
6. Dietrich Bonhoeffer, *Life Together* (New York: Harper & Row, 1954), 20–39.
7. Ibid.
8. By a community he means the place he moved into and lives in, not commuting to daily as if it were a "less desirable" place to live but for work is acceptable.
9. Hugh Prather, as cited in Job and Shawchuck, *The Quiet Answer* (New York: Doubleday, 1991), 276.
10. Carlo Carretto, *The God Who Comes* (Maryknoll, N.Y.: Orbis Books, 1974).

Chapter 10

1. Fred H. Wight, *Manners and Customs of Bible Lands* (Chicago: Moody, 1953).
2. Ibid.
3. Mother Francis Dominica, prayer.
4. Carretto, *The God Who Comes*, as cited in Job and Shawchuck, 15.
5. Shawchuck and Job, 275.

Chapter 11

1. Marlo Schalesky, "Remember Eve," *Discipleship Journal* (January–February 1995): 37.
2. I must mention that nearly two years following Evon's death and prior to my remarriage to Stephanie, I received a letter from that senior pastor. In it he shared how excited he was to see God moving healthily in my life. He also wrote, "Forgive me

for any pain I caused you . . . I felt like we were dealing with a monster so big, none of us knew how to handle it."

3. Herman, *Faith Quake*, 117.

4. *Webster's Collegiate Dictionary*, 10th ed., 844.

5. Lewis B. Smedes, *Forgive and Forget: Healing the Hurts We Don't Deserve* (New York: Harper & Row, 1984), xi.

6. Smedes, *Forgive and Forget*, 3–19.

7. Ibid., 18.

8. Ibid., 20.

9. Ibid.

10. Ibid., 27.

11. Ibid., 29.

12. Ibid., 36.

13. Edythe Draper, *Draper's Book of Quotations for the Christian World* (Wheaton: Tyndale House).

14. Smedes, *Forgive and Forget*, 82ff.

15. Richard Foster, *Celebration of Disciplines* (New York: HarperCollins, 1988), 143.

16. Smedes, "Postlude," *Forgive and Forget*.

17. Adapted from Frederick Buechner's prayers in *The Hungering Dark*, 69.

Chapter 12

1. Archaeologists have found fragments of pottery not only with memos and merchant records but also with portions of Scripture on them.

2. J. I. Packer, Merrill C. Tenney, William White Jr., *Nelson's Illustrated Encyclopedia of Bible Facts* (Nashville: Thomas Nelson, 1980).

3. The name Adam is a pun on the similar Hebrew words for "soil" and for "man." The word *Adam* is derived from the Hebrew word for "man" in the collective sense, as in humanity or mankind. It is also related to the Hebrew word *adamah*, which means "ground" or "earth." The author of Genesis used a wordplay. *Adam*, man, came from *adamah*, the ground.

4. Remen, *My Grandfather's Blessings*, 199.

Conclusion

1. James Orr, ed., *The International Standard Bible Encyclopedia*, vol. 2 (Grand Rapids: Eerdmans, 1930), 125.

2. Kay Arthur, *Lord, I Want to Know You* (Tarrytown, N.Y.: Revell, 1984), 43–48.

3. Brennan Manning, *Abba's Child: The Cry of the Heart for Intimate Belonging* (Colorado Springs: NavPress, 1994), 124–25.

4. MacRina Wiederkehr, *A Tree Full of Angels: Seeing the Holy in the Ordinary* (reprint; San Francisco: Harper SanFrancisco, 1995).

5. Richard M. Gula, *To Walk Together Again* (Mahwah, N.J.: Paulist Press, 1984).

6. Wiederkehr, *A Tree Full of Angels*.

7. Allender and Longman, *The Cry of the Soul*, 258.

8. Ibid.

9. I don't believe artists have truly grasped the magnitude of Jesus' beatings. If we could see his body today, we would see scars covering his brow, across his face, neck

and shoulders, his back, and upper thighs. Cruel beatings ravaged his flesh. The scars on the body of Christ depicting for us his history. His future was not determined by the scars but by God's plan and Jesus' desire to follow it. Interestingly Jesus is the only one in heaven whose body will forever be scarred.

10. Carlo Carretto, *Letters from the Desert* (Maryknoll, N.Y.: Orbis Books, 1982).

11. Allender and Longman, *The Cry of the Soul*, 258.

12. Claus Westermann, *The Living Psalms* (Grand Rapids: Eerdmans, 1989).

13. Carretto, *Why, O Lord?*

14. William Barclay, *Prayers for the Christian Year.*

Doug Herman is an international speaker and author who has spent over twenty years in youth and family work. Forums in which he has displayed his speaking ability include school systems, businesses, parent and family conferences, fund-raising banquets, and religious organizations and events.

Currently, Doug speaks to over 250,000 teens and adults yearly about character development, sexual abstinence, and spiritual passion. He is the founder of Integrated Community Events, Inc., a non-profit organization linking community networks for strategic efforts. The Pure Revolution Project is one of those efforts created by Doug to bring the message of sexual postponement until marriage to students, families, and communities.

Doug has been a youth pastor at small country churches as well as one of the nation's largest multicultural churches. His experience as a high school coach and substitute teacher has aided his effectiveness in the high school assembly programs he conducts nationally every year. Doug has been seen and heard on over 100 various national radio and television programs and has published articles in *Leadership Journal, Youthworker, Living with Teenagers,* and *ParentLife*.

Doug's new radio program, *Pure Revolution,* debuted in June 2002 on 313 stations. To learn more, visit Doug's web site: www.purerevolution.com.

*Leading generations
into a revolution of purity.*